Brazil

Brazil

BY ANN HEINRICHS

Enchantment of the World™
Second Series

CHILDREN'S PRESS®

An Imprint of Scholastic Inc.

New York   Toronto   London   Auckland   Sydney
Mexico City   New Delhi   Hong Kong
Danbury, Connecticut

Frontispiece: **Do Meio beach, Fernando de Noronha island**

Consultant: John Tofik Karam, PhD, Associate Professor, Latin American/Latino Studies Program, DePaul University, Chicago, Illinois

Please note: All statistics are as up-to-date as possible at the time of publication.

Book production by The Design Lab

Library of Congress Cataloging-in-Publication Data
Heinrichs, Ann.
  Brazil / by Ann Heinrichs.
       pages cm.—(Enchantment of the world. Second series)
  Includes bibliographical references and index.
  ISBN 978-0-531-23675-8 (lib. bdg.)
  1. Brazil—Juvenile literature. I. Title.
  F2508.5.H453 2013
  981—dc23   2013000089

1 2 3 4 5 6 7 8 9 10 R 23 22 21 20 19 18 17 16 15 14

Carnival performer

Contents

Left to right: **Christ the Redeemer, Iguaçu Falls, harvesting coconuts, capoeira, soccer**

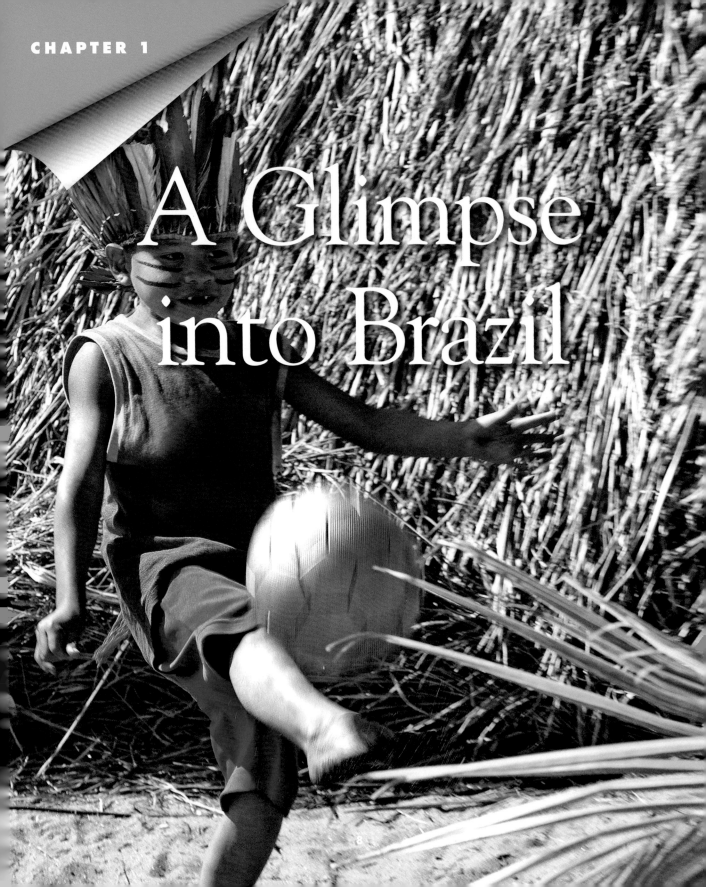

CHAPTER 1

A Glimpse into Brazil

PAULINHO IS UP AT 6:30 A.M. AND OUT THE DOOR AT 7:00. It's just a short walk to school, which begins at 7:15. Along the way, he meets his classmates, all wearing the same school uniform—a T-shirt with the school's name on it.

Paulinho is in fifth grade at his public school in São Paulo, Brazil. He starts his school day in the computer lab. Then he has Portuguese language and history classes. At 10:00, there's a short break for a lunch of rice, beans, vegetables, a banana, and guava juice. Next is science class, Paulinho's favorite. He loves animals, especially his pet frog, and he wants to become a zoologist, or animal scientist. Before noon, school is over for the day.

Paulinho races out for a game of soccer with his friends. With every kick of the ball come memories of the last World Cup soccer tournament and dreams of the next one. It is the world's premier international soccer competition, and Brazil has won it five times, more times than any other nation.

Opposite: **Children all over Brazil love soccer.**

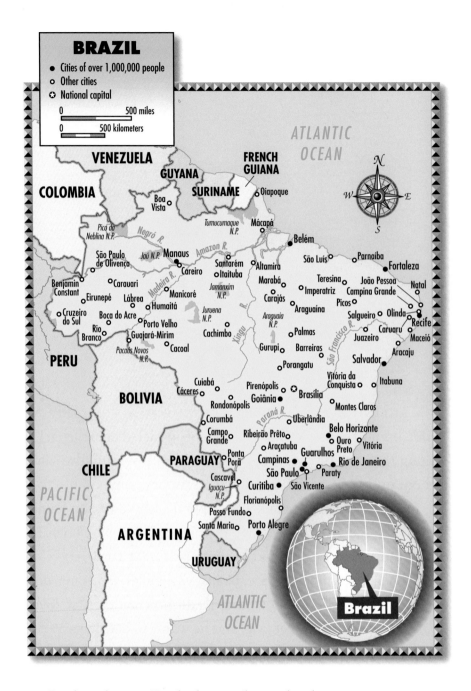

BRAZIL

- ● Cities of over 1,000,000 people
- ○ Other cities
- ✪ National capital

0   500 miles

0   500 kilometers

VENEZUELA

COLOMBIA

GUYANA

SURINAME

FRENCH GUIANA

ATLANTIC OCEAN

Boa Vista

Oiapoque

Picá da Neblina N.P.

Negró R.

Tumucumaque N.P.

Mácapá

São Paulo de Olivença

Jaú N.P.

Manaus

Amazon R.

Santarém

Itaituba

Altamira

Belém

São Luís

Parnaíba

Fortaleza

Benjamin Constant

Caravari

Careiro

Madeira R.

Manicoré

Jamanxim N.P.

Marabá

Imperatriz

Teresina

Campina Grande

João Pessoa

Natal

Eirunepé

Lábrea

Humaitá

Carajás

Araguaína

Picos

Salgueiro

Olinda

Recife

Cruzeiro do Sul

Boca do Acre

Juruena N.P.

Juruá R.

Xingu R.

Porto Velho

Cachimbo

Araguaia N.P.

Palmas

Caruaru

Juazeiro

Maceió

Rio Branco

Guajará-Mirim

Cacoal

Gurupi

Barreiras

São Francisco R.

Salvador

Aracaju

Pacaás Novos N.P.

PERU

Porangatu

Vitória da Conquista

Itabuna

BOLIVIA

Cuiabá

Cáceres

Pirenópolis

Goiânia

Brasília

Montes Claros

Rondonópolis

Corumbá

Paraná R.

Uberlândia

Belo Horizonte

Campo Grande

Ribeirão Prêto

Ouro Prêto

Vitória

Araçatuba

Guarulhos

Ponta Porã

Campinas

Rio de Janeiro

PARAGUAY

São Paulo

Paraty

Cascavel

Iguaçu N.P.

Curitiba

São Vicente

CHILE

PACIFIC OCEAN

Florianópolis

Passo Fundo

Santa Maria

Porto Alegre

ARGENTINA

URUGUAY

ATLANTIC OCEAN

Brazil

Back at home, Paulinho works on his history assignment. He is writing an essay on Pedro Álvares Cabral, the first European to reach Brazil. After a nap, some computer games, and a late-evening dinner, it's time for bed.

From his bedroom, Paulinho can smell spicy aromas drifting from the kitchen. His mother is preparing food for relatives who will visit next week. They're coming for the Feast of Our Lady of Aparecida. Devotions on this day focus on an image of Jesus's mother, Mary, who is the patron saint of Brazil. Like Paulinho, the three-hundred-year-old clay statue of Mary in São Paulo's cathedral has dark skin.

Each year on October 12, the Feast of Our Lady of Aparecida, more than one hundred thousand pilgrims wait in line to see the small statue of Mary.

Like most Brazilians, Paulinho has Indian, European, and African ancestors. His ethnic mix reflects his country's history. Brazil's native, or indigenous, people lived in the region for thousands of years before Europeans landed on its shores. After Cabral arrived from Portugal in 1500, the Portuguese made Brazil its colony. They brought in enslaved Africans to work their farms, ranches, and mines. These three ethnic groups blended together to produce a unique Brazilian culture.

Spanish is the dominant language in most of South America, but Brazilians speak Portuguese. For all countries in South America, though, Roman Catholicism is the major religion. Paulinho, like his city, is named after Saint Paul. Many of Brazil's religious holidays, such as Our Lady of Aparecida, are also national holidays.

Girls at a school in Rio de Janeiro. About one-quarter of the Brazilian population is under age fifteen.

Paulinho's school lunch reveals even more about his country. Although Brazil's economy is one of the largest in the world, and Brazil is the fifth most populated country in the world, millions of Brazilians suffer from extreme poverty. To improve conditions, Brazil provides for free, nutritious lunches in all public schools.

The banana and guava in Paulinho's lunch may have come from Brazil's Amazon rain forest. This dense tangle of tropical trees and vines is the largest rain forest in the world. Monkeys and tropical birds abound there, and no place on Earth has more species of living things. Paulinho knows the Amazon's animal and plant life are shrinking by the day. He hopes that when he becomes a zoologist, he can help preserve the forest's wildlife. As Paulinho drifts off to sleep, he imagines every detail of his favorite dream—discovering a new species of Amazon frog!

Toucans are among the brightest birds in the rain forest. Their large, colorful bills can be nearly half the length of their bodies.

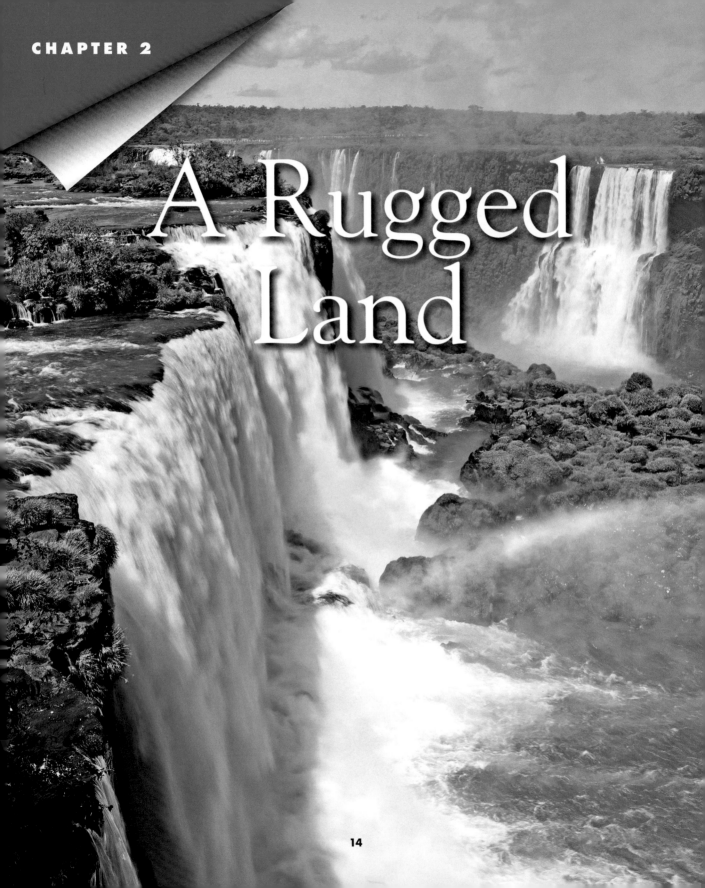

CHAPTER 2

A Rugged Land

IMAGINE YOU ARE AN EAGLE SOARING HIGH IN THE skies above Brazil. As you survey the landscape below, you see lush forests and barren deserts, emerald grasslands and murky swamps, glistening beaches, and rivers curling like snakes through the greenery.

Brazil is a beautiful and rugged land. It is the largest country on the continent of South America. The waters of the Atlantic Ocean lap against the shore along its eastern edge. Brazil's coastline is one of the world's longest, stretching about 4,650 miles (7,480 kilometers). Hundreds of inlets and bays cut into the ragged coast, and many islands lie offshore. Brazil's sparkling beaches attract visitors from all over the world.

Brazil borders ten other nations in South America. In fact, it touches every other country in South America except Ecuador and Chile. Venezuela, Guyana, Suriname, and French Guiana border Brazil on the north. To the northwest is Colombia, and to the west are Peru and Bolivia. Paraguay and Argentina are southwest of Brazil, and Uruguay borders the south.

Opposite: **Iguaçu Falls, on the border of Brazil and Argentina, is one of the largest waterfalls in the world. The falls are about 1.7 miles (2.7 km) long.**

Brazil's Geographic Features

Area: 3,287,612 square miles (8,514,876 sq km)

Highest Elevation: Neblina Peak (right), 9,888 feet (3,014 m) above sea level

Lowest Elevation: Sea level along the coast

Greatest Distance, North to South: 2,731 miles (4,395 km)

Greatest Distance, East to West: 2,684 miles (4,319 km)

Longest River: Amazon River (below), about 4,000 miles (6,400 km) overall, and about 1,960 miles (3,154 km) within Brazil

Highest Waterfall: Iguaçu Falls, 237 feet (72 m)

Average High Temperature: In Rio de Janeiro, 85°F (29°C) in January; 78°F (25°C) in July

Average Low Temperature: In Rio de Janeiro, 74°F (23°C) in January; 65°F (18°C) in July

Average Annual Rainfall: 46 inches (117 cm) in Rio de Janeiro; more than 160 inches (400 cm) in the western Amazon

Northern Brazil

The vast Amazon rain forest covers most of northern Brazil. More animal and plant species live in this lush forest than anywhere else in the world. Manaus and Belém are the largest cities in this region, and both owe their importance to the mighty Amazon River. Manaus, the region's major city, sits near the juncture of the Amazon and the Negro River. Belém lies near the mouth of the Amazon.

Along Brazil's northern border are the rugged Guiana Highlands. Neblina Peak (Mist Peak) is one of the many mountain peaks reaching up into the clouds. At 9,888 feet (3,014 meters), it is the highest point in the country.

The Amazon rain forest is thick with trees, vines, and shrubs.

Looking at Brazil's Cities

São Paulo (right), Brazil's largest city, is the nation's financial and industrial center. Catholic missionaries founded the city in 1554. By the 1800s, the region was the world's largest coffee producer, and São Paulo's wealthy coffee barons beautified the city with grand homes and spacious parks. In the early 1900s, the city was the center of a booming industrial region, and immigrants from many countries poured in to get jobs. Their descendants make São Paulo one of the most ethnically diverse cities in Brazil. A public square called the Praça da Sé is the hub of the bustling downtown area. Skyscrapers housing banks and other financial companies line the Avenida Paulista. São Paulo is the seventh-largest city in the world. Its population in 2012 was 11,376,685, and its metropolitan area, counting the surrounding suburbs, was almost 20 million.

Portuguese settlers founded Rio de Janeiro (below) in 1565, and sugarcane and gold from other parts of the country made the city's colonial rulers fabulously wealthy. Besides being Brazil's second-largest city, Rio de Janeiro, often known as Rio, is the most visited spot in South America. Rio's attractions include the towering Christ the Redeemer statue atop Corcovado Mountain, beaches such as Ipanema and Copacabana, the mas-

sive Maracanã Stadium, the cable car to the summit of Sugar Loaf Mountain, and the spectacular parades during the annual Carnival festivities. Among the city's many cultural landmarks are the National Library, the Botanical Garden, the National Museum of Fine Arts, the National Historical Museum, the Imperial Palace, and the cone-shaped Metropolitan Cathedral. In 2012, Rio had a population of 6,390,290, with more than 12 million residents in the metropolitan area.

Salvador, Brazil's third-largest city, is the capital of Bahia state. Located on a peninsula on the northeast coast, it has a population of 2,710,965 residents and a metropolitan population of about 3.6 million. Geographically, Salvador is divided into an upper city, on a higher elevation, and a lower city. People can ride between the two levels in large elevators. Salvador was Brazil's first colonial capital, founded in 1549. Today the Pelourinho district is known for its historic Portuguese architecture, including the Cathedral of Salvador, the Convent and Church of São Francisco, and the Church of Nosso Senhor do Bonfim. Brazil's African heritage is most visible in Salvador because of the thousands of enslaved Africans brought there in colonial times. African influence appears in the city's spicy foods, candomblé religious ceremonies, Afro-Brazilian music, and the martial art of capoeira.

The Northeast

The northeast is Brazil's hottest, driest region. Beaches, tropical forests, and fertile soils line the coastal plains. But farther inland is an arid plain called the sertão. Though the soil is not rich, some Brazilians farm and ranch there. The northeast is Brazil's poorest region, and farmers can barely scratch out a living in the bleak environment.

The northeast was the first region in what is now Brazil where Portuguese settled in the 1500s. Salvador, the first colonial capital, is today the region's largest city. Next in size are Fortaleza and Recife. All three lie along the coast.

The Central and Southern Plateaus

The Brazilian Highlands cover much of central and southern Brazil. This is a rugged region of rolling hills and high, flat plateaus. The highlands also include extensive grasslands where millions of cattle graze. Brasília, the capital city, was built in this

The highlands of central Brazil are broken by the rugged cliffs of Chapada dos Guimarães National Park.

More than six hundred kinds of birds live in the Pantanal, including herons, ibises, and jabiru storks (above).

region. In west-central Brazil is an immense swamp called the Pantanal, which spills over the border into Bolivia and Paraguay. This wetland is home to hundreds of species of waterbirds.

The southeast is Brazil's most populated region. Three of the country's largest cities—São Paulo, Rio de Janeiro, and Belo Horizonte—are located in this part of the country. Farms, ranches, mines, and factories in the southeast produce almost half the country's economic wealth.

The cattle ranches of southern Brazil are known for their *gaúchos*, or cowboys. Many romantic legends surround the gaúchos, though they have a very real working life today.

The most spectacular natural feature in southern Brazil is Iguaçu. This magnificent, horseshoe-shaped waterfall is almost three times as wide as Niagara Falls in North America. The Iguaçu River forms the falls as it plunges over cliffs on Brazil's border with Argentina.

The Amazon River

The Amazon is the major river in South America. It is also the second-longest river in the world, after the Nile River in Africa. The Amazon begins its course high in the Andes Mountains of Peru. Its waters cross the entire width of Brazil, emptying at last into the Atlantic Ocean.

The Amazon is a massive river. It carries about one-fifth of all the water in all the rivers of the world. The Amazon has many widely branching tributaries, smaller rivers that empty into it. These tributaries give the Amazon the world's largest drainage basin. This is the expanse of land whose waters eventually flow into the river. The Amazon Basin covers about 2.7 million square miles (7 million square kilometers).

The Amazon River meanders all the way across Brazil.

The Amazon River's two largest tributaries are the Madeira and the Negro Rivers. The Madeira River is the Amazon's longest tributary. It enters the Amazon from the south. The Negro River, meaning Black River, enters the Amazon from the north. Its dark color comes from decaying plant material picked up along its course. The Amazon and the Negro meet near Manaus, and their light and dark colors swirl together. This place is sometimes called the Marriage of the Waters. Brazilians call the section of the Amazon before this meeting point the Solimões River.

A man dives into the Amazon at the point where its light waters meet the dark waters of the Negro River.

Climate

Brazil is in the Southern Hemisphere, so its seasons are the opposite of those in the Northern Hemisphere. Brazil's summer lasts roughly from December through March. This is during the wet season, when the most rain falls in the country, and the Amazon and many other rivers flood. Winter, which occurs during the dry season, lasts from June through September. These dates vary a little from one region to another. However, for much of Brazil, January and February are the warmest months, and July and August are the coolest.

Most of Brazil lies within the tropical zone. This is the region nearest to the equator, an imaginary line that circles the earth an equal distance from the North and South Poles. The equator crosses northern Brazil, running through the mouth of the Amazon River. In general, northern Brazil gets warmer temperatures than the southern part of the country.

Many factors besides location affect Brazil's climate. One factor is altitude. Temperatures along the low-lying coastal plains are often very warm. Salvador, on the central coast, has an average annual temperature of 77 degrees Fahrenheit (25 degrees Celsius). The climate is much milder in cities high on the plateau, such as São Paulo, Brasília, and Belo Horizonte. Brasília's average temperature is 69°F (21°C).

The northeast is Brazil's hottest region. Temperatures in the inland sertão often rise higher than 100°F (38°C). This is also Brazil's driest region. Some parts of the sertão may go years without any rain.

In the south, summers are warm, but winter temperatures often dip below freezing. Snow sometimes falls in this region and in Brazil's mountains and high plateaus.

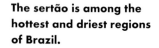

The sertão is among the hottest and driest regions of Brazil.

Climate Change and the Amazon

Vehicles and industrial plants pour tons of carbon dioxide (CO_2) and other chemicals into the air. These pollutants, called greenhouse gases, trap heat within Earth's atmosphere. This is affecting Earth's climate, causing changes in weather patterns and rising temperatures and sea levels.

The world's rain forests help slow down the process of climate change. They soak up about one-fifth of the world's greenhouse gas emissions. The Amazon rain forest is one of Earth's largest carbon sinks. That means it is a place that absorbs more CO_2 than it releases. The Amazon's trees and other plants take in about 1.7 billion tons of CO_2 every year and give off oxygen. Thus, the rain forest helps recycle Earth's air and keep it clean.

However, greenhouse gas emissions are rising, and the Amazon rain forest is shrinking. Loggers are cutting trees, and farmers want more land so they are clearing parts of the forest by burning it. As the Amazon rain forest shrinks, it could have a serious impact on climate conditions around the planet.

Most of Brazil gets a moderate amount of rainfall. The heaviest rains fall in the Amazon region, where it rains year-round. The western part of the Amazon gets more than 160 inches (400 centimeters) of rain every year. Newcomers to the Amazon notice how humid, or moist, the air is. They say they don't mind the heat, but the humidity makes them uncomfortable. The Amazon's humidity is due partly to rainwater evaporating. Much of it is also due to transpiration, a process in which leaves and other plant parts give off water vapor.

CHAPTER 3

Into the Wild

BRAZIL IS A PARADISE FOR NATURE LOVERS. EXPLORING the Amazon rain forest, they can find a spectacular array of plants and animals. No other place on the planet has as many wildlife species. In fact, the Amazon is home to almost 30 percent of all the plant and animal species in the world.

Scientists studying the forest have counted as many as three thousand types of trees in just 1 square mile (2.6 sq km). The numbers are just as amazing for animals. More than 1,500 bird species and more than 1,000 frog species inhabit this lush environment. From frisky monkeys to stealthy jaguars to slithering snakes, each species depends on many others for its survival. The rain forest is a vibrant ecosystem—a community of creatures linked together with all the elements of their environment.

Rain Forest Plants

The rain forest features many fascinating plants. Epiphytes, also called air plants, sprout from tree trunks and branches. They sink their roots into the rotting leaves and animal

Opposite: **Golden lion tamarins have bright orange fur. They live only in a few coastal forests near Rio de Janeiro.**

A small frog peeks out of a bromeliad. Bromeliads are a vital habitat in the Brazilian rain forest.

droppings that build up on the trees. These roots are just for support, though. Epiphytes get their nutrients from the air, rainwater, and decaying plant material on the tree. Epiphytes in the Amazon include orchids and ferns.

Bromeliads are flowering plants related to the pineapple. They have thick, waxy leaves that form a bowl shape in the center where rainwater collects. A type of tank bromeliad can hold 12 gallons (45 liters) of water. Insects and small animals can spend their entire lives in and around this pool. Some frog species lay their eggs there. The tadpoles hatch and grow up in the pool. Scientists have counted hundreds of tiny plant and animal species living in one bromeliad pool. Most bromeliads in the Amazon are also epiphytes and are attached to trees, but some root in the ground.

Thick, woody vines called lianas wind around trunks and branches. They are rooted in the soil, from which they absorb nutrients. Lianas can grow thousands of feet long, sometimes stretching from one tree to another. Monkeys use lianas to swing from tree to tree.

Creatures of the Forest Floor

If you were to trek through the rain forest, you might have trouble seeing where you were going. The forest floor is so dark that travelers sometimes need flashlights or lanterns to light their way! That is because the treetops block the sunlight,

National Tree

The *pau-brasil*, or brazilwood tree, is Brazil's national tree. Portuguese explorer Pedro Álvares Cabral sent a shipload of brazilwood trunks back to Portugal in 1500 to show how valuable Brazil's products were. This tropical hardwood secretes a bright red substance used as a dye. For years, it was the main source of red dye for the luxurious red clothing popular in the royal French court. The wood itself was often crafted into violin bows. Brazilwood trees grow in the sandy soil along Brazil's coast.

Into the Wild **29**

so very little light reaches the ground. This shadowy zone is home to many fascinating creatures.

Capybaras, the world's largest rodents, are related to guinea pigs but look something like big, hairy pigs. They graze on grasses and eat fallen fruits and tree bark. Capybaras are social animals, living in packs of ten to twenty. They seem to vocalize constantly, emitting an amazing variety of barks, chirps, purrs, and whistles. When they are hiding from predators, they can stay underwater for up to five minutes.

Giant anteaters have a small head and a long snout.

Capybaras get their name from a Tupi Indian word meaning "grass eater." Capybaras eat only plants—primarily grass and aquatic plants.

Inside is a long tongue that can stick out more than 2 feet (0.6 m). The anteater can flick that tongue into an anthill or a termite mound up to 160 times a minute. In just one day, an anteater licks up as many as thirty-five thousand insects.

The tapir has a long snout, too. Tapirs can move their snout around to help them grab leaves, fruits, and grasses to eat. Tapirs often sleep on riverbanks and leap into the water to escape predators.

Any of these animals could become a meal for a jaguar. Jaguars stalk their prey by creeping along the ground or on a low tree branch. Then they spring out and pounce, sometimes using their powerful jaws to crack their prey's skull. The jaguar is one of the Amazon's many endangered species. Many poachers, or illegal hunters, make a good living by selling high-priced jaguar skins. Brazil's federal police and environmental officials have the often-dangerous task of hunting down the poachers. The goal, perhaps impossible, is to put poachers out of business forever.

Jaguars eat only meat. They prey on many animals, but prefer large species such as deer, tapirs, and foxes.

Healing Plants

Many of today's medicines were derived from plants found in the Amazon rain forest. Scientists believe that many more healing substances are yet to be found there. The Amazon's indigenous people traditionally used many different plants for medicinal purposes.

The cat's claw is a woody vine with thorns that look like hooks or claws. It stimulates the immune system, reduces swelling, and protects the body's cells. Indigenous people have used cat's claw to ease joint pain, cure deep wounds, reduce fever, and treat tumors.

The Brazilian peppertree is a shrubby tree with small flowers that bear clusters of berries (left). Native people have used it to heal wounds, stop bleeding, treat toothaches, and relieve depression. Scientists have found that various parts of the peppertree kill bacteria and even some cancer cells.

Annatto (above) is a shrubby tree with a profusion of seedpods. Its crushed seeds produce a yellow-orange substance that can be used as body paint or fabric dye. Some indigenous people use the leaves and other plant parts to treat skin problems, fever, liver disease, heartburn, and digestive problems.

The Canopy Community

The canopy layer of the rain forest is like a leafy roof. It consists of treetops reaching toward the sunlight. Canopy trees grow 80 feet (25 m) or more in height. They include Brazil nut, fig, rubber, mahogany, and palm trees. Their branches are home to most of the rain forest's creatures—monkeys, frogs, sloths, snakes, birds, and even some small cat species. The canopy is a flurry of motion, with animals jumping, flying, and gliding among the treetops. The canopy is noisy, too, filled with chattering monkeys and screeching birds.

Almost one hundred species of monkeys live in the Amazon. They eat fruit, nuts, leaves, insects, and birds' eggs. Most Amazon monkeys have prehensile tails—that is, tails that can curl around and grasp a branch. A prehensile tail is like a fifth limb that helps the monkey swing from branch to branch. Monkeys that inhabit the canopy include spider monkeys, howler monkeys, squirrel monkeys, marmosets, and tamarins.

Spider monkeys are named for their long, spidery arms and legs. They rarely leave the canopy for the forest floor because they are clumsy when walking. Howler monkeys are the largest Amazon monkeys and the loudest land animals on earth. Marmosets are tiny monkeys with claws on their feet. The pygmy marmoset, the smallest monkey in the world, is only about 6 inches (15 cm) long, not counting its tail. Tamarins are a type of marmoset. The golden lion tamarin has a silky, reddish-gold mane, like a lion's mane. This monkey is highly endangered because it is hunted for its fur.

Birds such as toucans and parrots add brilliant colors to the canopy. Toucans have banana-shaped bills that may be yellow, orange, green, blue, or multicolored. They sleep with that huge bill tucked under one of their wings. Parrots have sharp, curved beaks for breaking nuts open. When they eat, they often stand on one foot and use the other foot to bring food to their mouth.

The largest type of parrot is the macaw, and many species are named for their colors. For example, there are scarlet, green, red-and-green, and blue-and-yellow macaws. Macaws live as long as sixty years, and they mate for life. Several macaw species are endangered, because their habitat is disappearing as the forest is cut down, and because they are trapped illegally to be sold as pets.

Three-toed sloths spend much of their time hanging upside down by their long, curved claws. They eat, sleep, and even give birth in this position. Opossums also sometimes hang by their tails. They forage for fruit and insects at night. The ring-tailed coatimundi is not a hanger, but it sleeps in the canopy at night. It feeds in the daytime, unlike its raccoon relatives.

Frogs, Snakes, and Caimans

Many forest predators eat frogs, but one frog is definitely not on the menu. It is the tiny poison dart, or poison arrow, frog. This little frog, only 1 inch (2.5 cm) long, is one of the most toxic, or poisonous, creatures on earth. Predators recognize it by its brilliant red, yellow, orange, or blue colors. The most dangerous species contains enough poison to kill at least ten adult humans or ten thousand mice. Indigenous people have used the toxic substance in its skin to poison the tips of their darts and arrows.

One of the most bizarre Amazon frogs is the tiny glass frog. It has transparent skin, so its bones and internal organs are plainly visible. Adults reach only about 1 inch (2.5 cm) long. On the other extreme, the huge Amazon horned frog can grow as long as 8 inches (20 cm). It eats almost anything. To hunt, it buries itself in the forest floor with only its head aboveground. When something passes by—snap! It swallows the unlucky prey whole and locks it in its mouth with its teeth. Horned frogs have been found dead with half-swallowed prey sticking out of their mouth.

More than two hundred species of snakes live in the Amazon. Boa constrictors and anacondas are the largest. Green anacondas are the subject of many terrifying Indian legends. They are one of the world's largest snake species, growing as long as 20 feet (6 m) or more. An anaconda coils itself around its prey to crush it. Then it swallows the animal whole. Anacondas have been known to swallow jaguars and wild pigs! It takes days for them to digest prey this big.

Brazil Nuts and Agoutis

Brazil nuts are encased in round, hard, woody pods that crash to the ground like cannonballs as they fall from trees. The agouti is the only animal with teeth sharp enough to chisel through the pods and expose the nuts. Like squirrels, agoutis bury the nuts around the forest floor. The nuts they forget to eat may grow into new trees.

Into the Wild **35**

The caiman is a relative of the alligator. Black caimans are becoming rare because they are hunted for their skins. Poachers go after caimans at night. They scan the riverbanks with flashlights until they see a caiman's shining pair of eyes.

Beyond the Amazon

Along Brazil's east coast, where the climate is drier, trees do not grow as tall as rain forest tree species. Many lose their leaves during the dry season. The first European colonists settled along the coast, and Indians showed them how to eat the tangy, pear-shaped fruit of the cashew tree. Hanging at the bottom of each fruit was a bonus—a savory cashew nut.

A butterfly lands on the nose of a black caiman in the Pantanal.

The Pantanal

Stretching across Brazil's west-central border, the Pantanal is one of the largest wetlands in the world. It extends into Paraguay and Bolivia, covering more than 68,000 square miles (180,000 sq km). Hundreds of animal species thrive in this marshy habitat. Among them are jaguars, capybaras, tapirs, caimans, giant river otters, bush dogs, and giant anteaters. One of the Pantanal's exotic waterbirds is the jabiru stork, which stands 5 feet (1.5 m) tall. Many cattle ranches are in the Pantanal region, and jaguars sometimes prey on the cattle. This often makes the endangered jaguar the target of illegal hunting.

A thorny type of shrub called *caatinga* covers much of the dry northeastern backlands of Brazil. Farther south, in central Brazil, is the *cerrado*, a region with hardy grasses and scrubby trees. More luxuriant grasslands cover the southeastern plateau.

Flowering bushes and trees add brilliant splashes of color to the southern highlands. Araucaria trees, or Paraná pines, grow there, too. The pine forests are quickly disappearing as they are cut for construction timber. Here, as in the rain forest, there is an ongoing struggle between two forces: industrial development and environmental protection.

Fortunately, Brazil's aggressive conservation measures have slowed the rate of deforestation. This, in turn, helps preserve the habitats of thousands of animal species. Nature lovers can only hope that they will always find a paradise in Brazil.

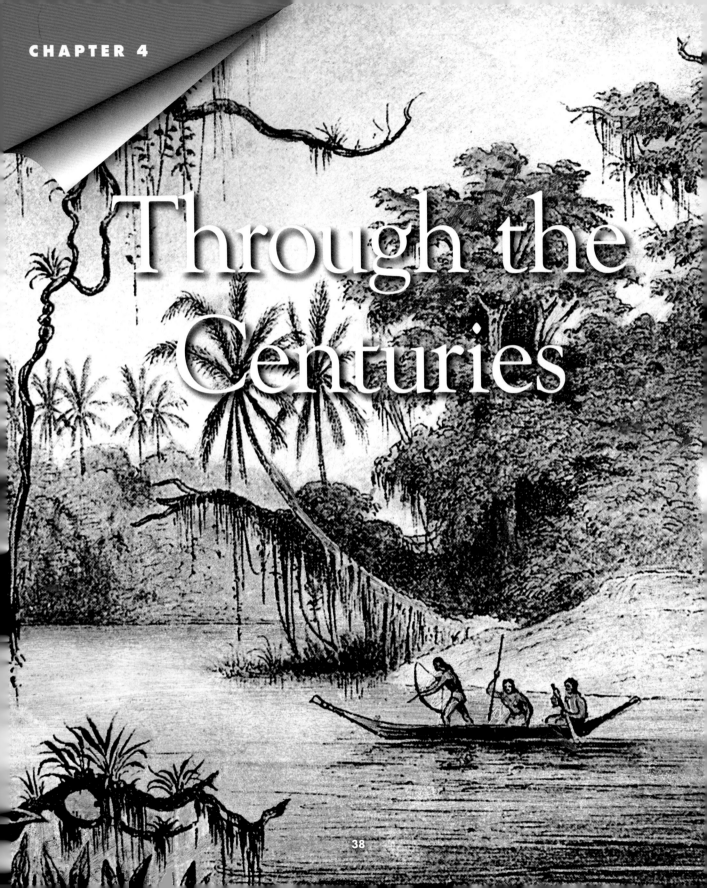

CHAPTER 4

Through the Centuries

EOPLE HAVE LIVED IN WHAT IS NOW BRAZIL SINCE at least 9000 BCE. Early inhabitants arrived in the Americas from Asia. They may have crossed a land bridge between eastern Asia and what is now the U.S. state of Alaska. Or, they may have sailed across the Pacific Ocean. Once they reached South America, various indigenous groups survived by hunting wild animals and fishing in the rivers and along the coasts. From the forests they gathered fruits, roots, and herbs. Some cultivated cassava, or manioc. This starchy root was their staple food. Maize (corn) was another important crop.

Some groups traveled from one settlement to another, depending on the seasons or the food supply. Others established villages of longhouses with thatched roofs made from forest foliage. One house sheltered several families, each with its own section. The people wove baskets, baked clay pottery, and fashioned utensils, tools, and weapons from wood and stone.

Opposite: **Traditionally, Indians in Brazil got much of their food from hunting and gathering wild plants.**

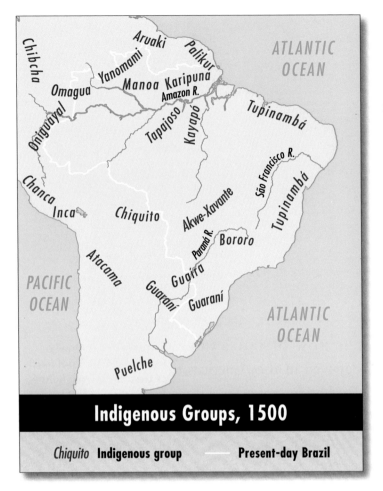

Indigenous Groups, 1500

Chiquito **Indigenous group** —— **Present-day Brazil**

Before 1500 CE, several million Indians lived in what is now Brazil. They were divided into as many as two thousand distinct ethnic groups. Among the major groups were the Tupi and the Guaraní. They were the first indigenous peoples the Europeans met.

Colonial Brazil

Portuguese navigator Pedro Álvares Cabral left Europe in 1500, headed for India. Instead of reaching India, he landed on the northeast coast of present-day Brazil. No one knows why or how Cabral ended up so far off course. He named the land Ilha de Vera Cruz (Island of the True Cross) and claimed it for Portugal. In time, Brazil would become Portugal's largest and wealthiest colony.

Brazilwood was the first Brazilian product shipped back to Europe. Its wood yielded a brilliant red liquid used to dye cloth. Portuguese colonists founded São Vicente, Brazil's first European settlement, in 1532 and Olinda in 1535. Portuguese missionaries soon arrived to convert Indians to Christianity. Missionaries founded São Paulo in 1554.

Gradually, the Portuguese expanded to the west. They cleared the land, drove Indians from their villages, and set up vast sugarcane plantations. By 1600, Brazil's top export was sugar. Miners made their fortunes in this new land, too. In the southern state of Minas Gerais, gold was discovered around 1695 and diamonds in 1729. Thousands of Portuguese and Africans mined the land.

Meanwhile, the lives of many Indians were in ruins. Many Indians were slaughtered while resisting the Portuguese. Others died of diseases such as measles and smallpox introduced by Europeans. The native people had never been exposed to these diseases before so their bodies had no natural resistance to them.

Colonists tried to force Indians to work as slave laborers on their plantations and in their mines, but the Indians fought back, and many fled. The Portuguese began bringing enslaved Africans to the colony to provide the labor. By 1700, almost a million Africans had been captured and shipped to Brazil. The Portuguese, Indians, and Africans had children together. In time, the mix of races, languages, and customs produced a unique Brazilian culture.

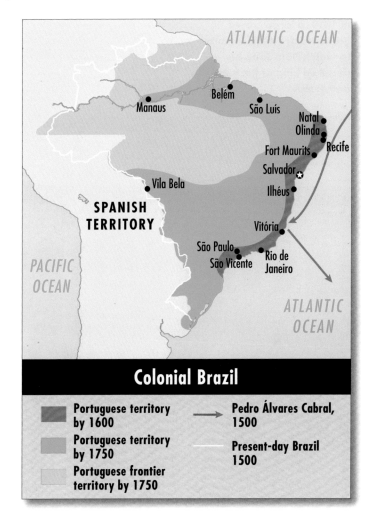

Colonial Brazil

- Portuguese territory by 1600
- Portuguese territory by 1750
- Portuguese frontier territory by 1750
- → Pedro Álvares Cabral, 1500
- — Present-day Brazil 1500

Independence

Events in Europe often had dramatic effects on Brazil. In 1807, Emperor Napoléon Bonaparte of France marched across Spain to invade Portugal. The royal family of Portugal had to escape. Together with hundreds of other Portuguese citizens, Dom João VI (King John VI) and his family boarded ships for Brazil. In 1808, the royal family settled in Rio de Janeiro and eventually named their empire the United Kingdom of Portugal, Brazil, and the Algarves (the southernmost part of what is now Portugal). This put Brazil on almost equal footing with Portugal. Over time, Brazilians were granted increasing freedoms and privileges.

In 1818, a large crowd gathered in Rio de Janeiro to watch Dom João be declared king of Portugal and Brazil.

Dom João VI returned to Portugal in 1821, leaving his son Pedro in charge of Brazil. Many Brazilians were afraid Portugal would take away their newfound freedoms. They wanted independence, and Pedro was wholeheartedly on their side. "I swear to give Brazil freedom," Pedro is said to have declared. "Independence or death!"

On September 7, 1822, Pedro declared Brazil's independence from Portugal. Its three centuries as a colony were over. Pedro became Emperor Pedro I of the Empire of Brazil.

The Empire of Brazil

Under Pedro I, the people of Brazil enjoyed civil rights, freedom of speech, a booming economy, and a two-house parliament with elected members. But turmoil in Portugal compelled Pedro to return there in 1831. He left his son Pedro II to rule in his place. The problem was that Pedro II was only five years old at the time. Weak politicians managed the government until 1841, when fifteen-year-old Pedro was crowned Emperor Pedro II.

Emperor Pedro II

Pedro II (1825–1891) did not have much of a childhood. His mother died when he was a year old, and his father left when he was five. To prepare him to rule Brazil, Pedro's guardians made him study from early morning until late at night. Little time was allowed for playing. Pedro was a shy and serious child who liked reading. Once he became emperor, he took his role seriously and became a strong leader. He supported the arts and sciences and promoted education. Pedro was forced from the throne in 1889. He then settled in Paris, France, where he died two years later.

During his forty-eight-year reign, Pedro II brought Brazil into the modern world. He started a public school system and built factories to turn cotton into cloth. Roads and railroads were built into the interior of the country, and steamships chugged up and down the Amazon. Speedy communication took place over new telegraph lines.

Shiploads of European settlers arrived to make their fortune. Many grew coffee in the rich, red soil around São Paulo. Brazil became the leading coffee producer in the world. Gold mines flourished in the interior, and a new rubber industry sprang up in the Amazon. Brazil was now exporting coffee, rubber, cacao (the beans used to make chocolate), and cattle.

Slavery Ends, a Republic Begins

Pedro II abolished the slave trade in 1850 and outlawed slavery altogether in 1888. Brazil was the last nation in the Western

Hemisphere to abolish slavery. This act led to Pedro's downfall. Brazil's powerful plantation owners hated to lose their slaves. With the army's help, they forced Pedro out of the country. On November 15, 1889, Brazil was declared a republic.

Pedro did not particularly care about losing his position. Although most of his subjects loved him, he did not like being an emperor and did not like the idea of an empire. He was pleased that he left behind a prosperous and cultured nation.

Manuel Deodoro da Fonseca, who headed the forces that ousted Pedro, became the republic's first president. Now Brazil attracted more immigrants than ever before. Many Brazilians did not want to hire the newly freed slaves and their descendants to work for them. Instead, they hired the German, Italian, and Japanese immigrants.

The Imperial Palace

The Imperial Palace is in the center of downtown Rio de Janeiro. It was completed in 1743 as the residence for Brazil's colonial governors. When Dom João of Portugal arrived in 1808, it became his home. Emperors Pedro I and Pedro II both lived and worked there. The outer walls of the palace enclose several courtyards. After the Republic of Brazil was established in 1889, the magnificent building was converted into Rio's central post office. Restoration began in the 1980s when the building was recognized as an important historical and architectural site. The Imperial Palace is now a cultural center with art exhibits, concerts, and a library housing rare books.

The Twentieth Century

Brazil's economy weakened in the early 1900s. Brazil's rubber industry collapsed as Southeast Asia became the world's biggest rubber supplier and artificial rubber was invented. Coffee then became Brazil's major export. When world coffee prices dropped, the economy suffered. The country became more chaotic. In 1930, army officers took over and made Getúlio Vargas, the governor of the state of Rio Grande do Sul, president.

By 1900, São Paulo was a thriving city of 240,000 people.

Working on coffee plantations was often hot, difficult work. Here, women hoe weeds around coffee seedlings.

Vargas came to power just as the Great Depression of the 1930s hit. During this worldwide economic downturn, businesses failed, and millions of Brazilians were out of work. To address the crisis, Vargas ruled as a dictator. His harsh measures helped Brazil out of its economic slump. He used his power to put people to work, building new schools, highways, and power plants. The nation saw improvements in health, education, transportation, and labor.

In 1960, President Juscelino Kubitschek built the new capital city of Brasília. Kubitschek also built roads and power plants, and encouraged steel, automobile, shipbuilding, and machinery industries. With business booming, rural people left their farms and swarmed into the cities to find jobs. There was not enough housing for all these newcomers, so they built *favelas*, or neighborhoods of ramshackle housing, on the outskirts of cities. Poverty and unemployment reached emergency levels.

In 1964, the army took over the government again. A military dictatorship was in power for the next twenty years. Military rulers took away the people's political rights and harshly suppressed any criticism of the government. By 1985, civilians had had enough. They overturned the military rule and declared the era of the New Republic.

The New Republic

Democracy had returned to Brazil at last. For the first time in decades, Brazilians were able to elect their own president, representatives, and state officials. The country now faced staggering economic problems. The government was deeply in debt to foreign banks, and prices were more than doubling every year. Brazil's presidents tried to fix these problems. Fernando

Henrique Cardoso, elected in 1994, cut government spending, introduced the *real* as Brazil's unit of currency, and began transferring government-run industries to private companies.

Cardoso also tackled some of Brazil's dire social issues. He improved rural health care, drastically reducing the rate of infant deaths. His reforms in the public school system led to much higher enrollments. Cardoso also helped the so-called landless peasants, or landless workers. These were people in the rural countryside who had no farmland. At the same time, large private estates owned millions of acres of land that

In the 1980s, Brazilians began holding large rallies demanding that poor Brazilians be given unused land to farm.

they did not use. Under his land reform measures, Cardoso resettled nearly six hundred thousand landless families on land they could call their own.

Luiz Inácio Lula da Silva, known as Lula, became president in 2003. Lula is often called the most popular politician in Brazil's history. He was a founding member of the Workers' Party, which favors trade unions and workers' rights. As a member of the working class himself, Lula was welcomed as someone who would help the poor. During his two terms as president, he created many new jobs, raised the minimum wage, and helped millions of Brazilians move out of poverty.

As president, Luiz Inácio Lula da Silva focused on programs to combat hunger and reduce poverty.

Lula's successor, Dilma Rousseff, became Brazil's first woman president in 2011. She had been Lula's minister of energy and chief of staff. One of Rousseff's main goals has been to improve life for Brazil's poorest citizens. She has also focused on attracting new business to Brazil. Rousseff has tried to keep a balance between economic development and environmental protection.

These issues have plagued Brazilians in the past and will not be resolved easily. Fortunately, the nation enjoys a stable government and a thriving economy. In 2012, when many countries were suffering the effects of a recession, Brazil's unemployment rate was below 6 percent. For a nation with a turbulent past, Brazil has every reason to expect a bright future.

President Dilma Rousseff speaks to Brazilian athletes in 2011.

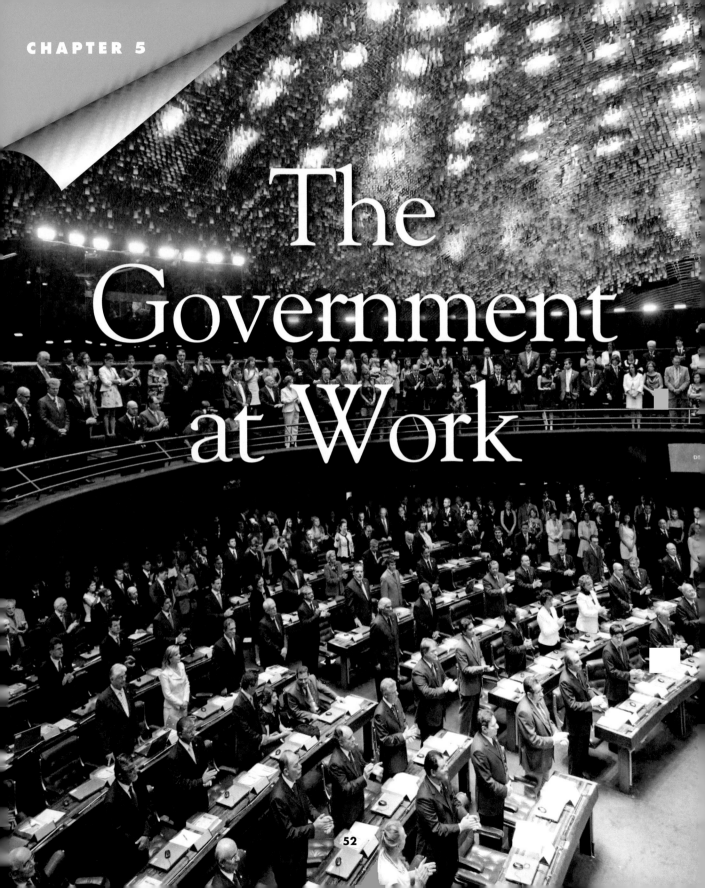

CHAPTER 5

The Government at Work

BRAZIL'S OFFICIAL NAME IS REPÚBLICA FEDERATIVA do Brasil, or the Federative Republic of Brazil. Under the present constitution, adopted in 1988, the nation has three branches of government. They are the executive, legislative, and judicial branches. The constitution also outlines how each branch is organized and how officeholders are elected.

Opposite: **Newly elected senators are sworn into office inside the senate chambers in Brasília.**

Executive Branch

The president is Brazil's head of state. The president and vice president are elected for four-year terms and may serve two terms in a row. The president appoints a cabinet made up of several ministers. They are in charge of areas such as foreign affairs, agriculture, mines and energy, culture, the environment, and tourism. Ministers report directly to the president.

Legislative Branch

Brazil's lawmaking body is the National Congress. It is composed of two chambers, or houses: the Chamber of Deputies and the Federal Senate.

The National Flag

The Brazilian flag features a large yellow diamond on a green background. In the diamond is a blue circle representing the starry night sky over Rio de Janeiro on November 15, 1889, the date Brazil was proclaimed a republic. Four days later, the republic officially adopted this flag. In the circle are twenty-seven stars, representing each of the Brazilian states and the Federal District. Across the blue circle is a white band inscribed with the national motto, *Ordem e Progresso* (Order and Progress).

The Chamber of Deputies includes 513 deputies. Each of the country's twenty-six states gets to elect a certain number of deputies, depending on that state's population. However, no state gets fewer than eight deputies or more than seventy, no matter how big or small its population is. For example, the northwestern state of Roraima, in the Amazon region, is the least-populated state in the country, with fewer than half a million residents. Nevertheless, it elects eight deputies. On the other extreme, the state of São Paulo has more than ninety times as many residents as Roraima. Still, it gets only seventy deputies. All deputies serve four-year terms.

The Senate is composed of eighty-one senators. Each state, plus the Federal District, elects three senators, no matter how large or small its population is. Senators serve eight-year terms. Federal deputies and senators can be reelected for any number of terms.

The music for "Hino Nacional Brasileiro" ("Brazilian National Anthem") was composed by Francisco Manuel da Silva in 1822. The lyrics, written in 1909 by Joaquim Osório Duque Estrada, were officially adopted in 1922.

Portuguese lyrics

Ouviram do Ipiranga às margens plácidas
De um povo heróico o brado retumbante,
E o sol da Liberdade, em raios fúlgidos,
Brilhou no céu da Pátria nesse instante.

Se o penhor dessa igualdade
Conseguimos conquistar com braço forte,
Em teu seio, ó Liberdade,
Desafia o nosso peito a própria morte!

Ó Pátria amada,
Idolatrada,
Salve! Salve!

Brasil, um sonho intenso, um raio vívido
De amor e de esperança à terra desce,
Se em teu formoso céu, risonho e límpido,
A imagem do Cruzeiro resplandece.

Gigante pela própria natureza,
És belo, és forte, impávido colosso,
E o teu futuro espelha essa grandeza.

Terra adorada, Entre outras mil,
És tu, Brasil,
Ó Pátria amada!

Dos filhos deste solo és mãe gentil,
Pátria amada, Brasil!

English translation

The peaceful banks of the Ipiranga
Heard the resounding cry of a heroic people,
And the dazzling rays of the sun of Liberty
Bathed our country in their brilliant light.

If with strong arm we have succeeded
In winning a pledge of equality,
In thy bosom, O Liberty,
Our hearts will defy death itself!

O adored Fatherland,
Cherished and revered,
All Hail! All Hail!

Brazil, a dream sublime, a vivid ray
Of love and hope to earth descends,
Where in your clear, pure, beauteous skies
The image of the Southern Cross shines forth.

O country vast by nature,
Fair and strong, a brave colossus,
Thy future mirrors this thy greatness.

O land adored above all others,
'Tis thee, Brazil,
Beloved fatherland!

Thou art the gentle mother of the children of this soil,
Beloved land, Brazil!

National Government of Brazil

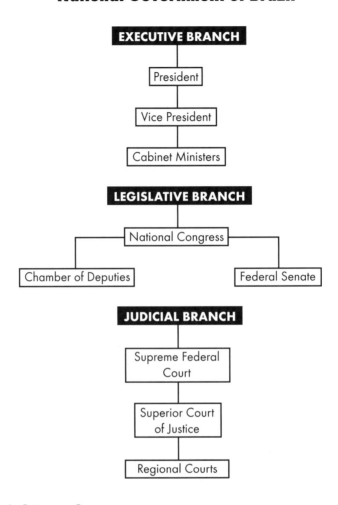

EXECUTIVE BRANCH

President

Vice President

Cabinet Ministers

LEGISLATIVE BRANCH

National Congress

Chamber of Deputies

Federal Senate

JUDICIAL BRANCH

Supreme Federal Court

Superior Court of Justice

Regional Courts

Judicial Branch

The top court in Brazil's justice system is the Supreme Federal Court. It is composed of eleven judges who meet in Brasília. The president appoints judges after a majority of the Senate has approved their nominations. This court's main role is to rule on issues that have to do with the constitution. That may include deciding whether a law is constitutional or whether the president has the constitutional right to do something.

The Capital City

Brasília became Brazil's capital city in 1960. It was built from scratch on a location in the center of the country. Thanks to city planner Lúcio Costa and architect Oscar Niemeyer, the city is a landmark of modern design. The basic street pattern is laid out in the form of a cross. The sweeping curve of the north-south line, however, is often said to look like the wings of an airplane or a bird.

Along the north-south axis are residential neighborhoods, each with its own parks, business centers, churches, and schools. Neighborhoods were designed to include both low-priced and expensive homes. The east-west line is called the Monumental Axis. At the east end, clustered

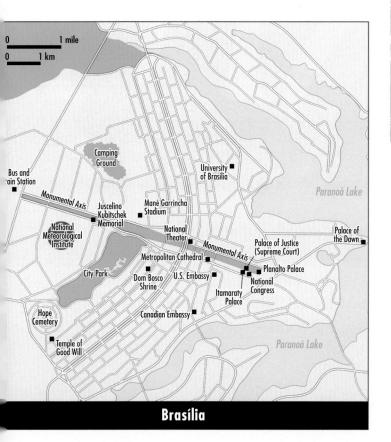

Brasília

around the Plaza of Three Powers, are the Planalto Palace, where the president's offices are located; the National Congress (top), with its dome- and bowl-shaped sections; and the Supreme Court, called the Palace of Justice.

Paranoá Lake curves around the eastern half of the city. On the tip of a peninsula jutting into the lake is the Palace of the Dawn, the president's magnificent residence. Another notable building is the circular Metropolitan Cathedral, which has curved pillars that sweep up into the shape of a crown.

Several other cities and towns have grown up around the central city. In 2012, Brasília's metropolitan area was home to about 3.7 million people, while the city itself had about 2.6 million residents.

Justice Joaquim Barbosa became the president of the Supreme Federal Court in 2012.

The Superior Court of Justice is the nation's top court for cases that do not concern the constitution. Its thirty-three judges also rule on cases involving state governors. Beneath this court are regional federal courts. There are also labor courts, electoral courts, and military courts.

Political Parties

Voters in the United States are used to choosing between two major political parties. In Brazil, voters support candidates in more than twenty political parties. This situation often forces candidates to cooperate with one another. To increase their chances of getting elected, two or more parties may join together and form a coalition.

Four of Brazil's political parties have the largest followings. The Brazilian Democratic Movement Party includes politicians with diverse viewpoints. The Workers' Party is a progressive party that was founded in 1980 as an opponent to the military dictatorship. Both former president Lula da Silva (2003–2010) and President Rousseff (2011–present) are members of the Workers' Party. The Brazilian Social Democracy Party is a center-left party. The Progressive Party is a conservative or center-right party.

Ms. President

Dilma Rousseff (1947–) became Brazil's first female president on January 1, 2011. Her path to the presidency was not easy. In the late 1960s she was part of a militant communist group, and in the early 1970s she was imprisoned and tortured for opposing Brazil's military dictatorship. Later, President Lula da Silva appointed her as his minister of mines and energy and then his chief of staff. After becoming president, Rousseff focused on domestic problems such as improving life for Brazil's poorest citizens. She is also known as a tough, no-nonsense leader. In 2012 *Forbes* magazine named Rousseff the world's third most powerful woman, after German chancellor Angela Merkel and then U.S. secretary of state Hillary Clinton.

Electoral System

Brazil is a pioneer in electronic voting. The country first tested electronic voting machines in 1996. By the 2000 elections, all voting was conducted electronically, even in the most remote regions of the country. This has ensured speedy vote counts.

In many countries, people may choose to not vote in elections. In Brazil, however, voting is required for all citizens between the ages of eighteen and seventy who can read and write. Voting is optional for sixteen- and seventeen-year-olds, people over seventy, and those who cannot read and write.

In presidential elections, each party chooses its candidate for president. Presidential elections take place in two rounds. All candidates run in the first round. Then the top two candidates from round one face each other in round two.

A woman casts her vote in Brasília. Although voting is mandatory, this rule is not enforced, and generally only about 80 percent of voters go to the polls.

Brazilian States

Local Government

Brazil is divided into twenty-six states and the federal district, the location of the capital city of Brasília. Citizens in each state elect a governor and a legislature. The states are divided into municipalities, which are something like counties in the United States, encompassing both urban and rural areas. Voters in the municipalities elect mayors and municipal councils.

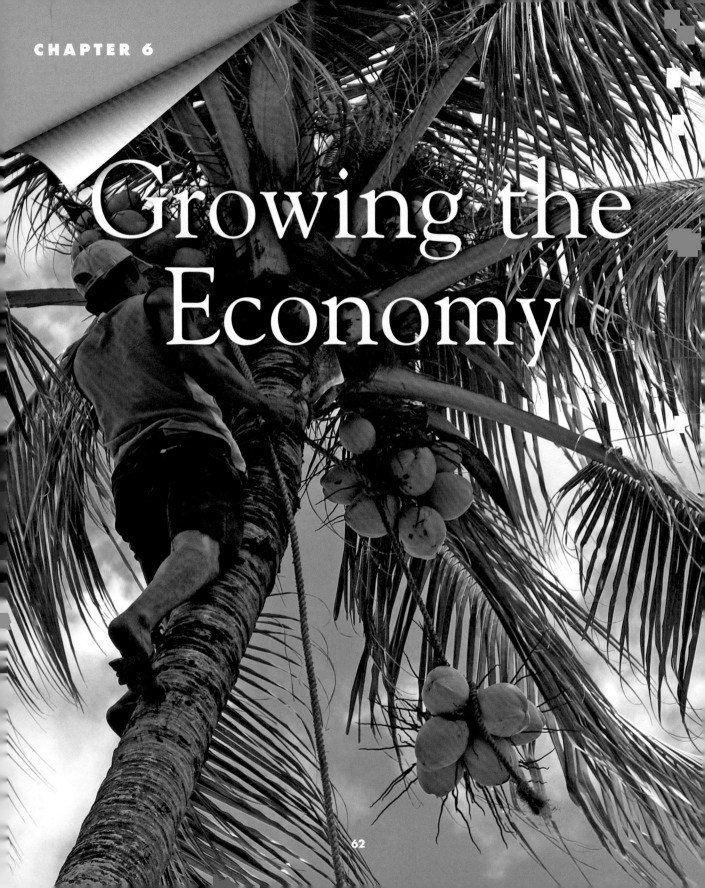

CHAPTER 6

Growing the Economy

BRAZIL IS KNOWN AS AN EMERGING ECONOMY. THAT means its businesses and industrial activity are growing fast. Economies are measured in terms of a country's gross domestic product (GDP)—the total value of all the goods and services produced in a year. In 2012, Brazil had the world's sixth-largest economy. The only countries ahead of Brazil economically were the United States, China, Japan, Germany, and France.

Opposite: **A man climbs a palm tree to harvest coconuts. Brazil is the world's fourth-largest producer of coconuts.**

Agriculture

The southern two-thirds of Brazil is its richest farming region. The soil is fertile, the climate is mild, and rainfall is plentiful. Farmers there grow the country's leading crops, such as coffee, sugarcane, and soybeans. Millions of cattle graze across the vast grasslands of central Brazil. From the Amazon region and other forestlands come tropical fruits, cocoa beans, and lumber.

Crops account for about three-fifths of the nation's farming output. Cattle and other livestock make up the rest. Brazil ranks number one in the world in production of coffee,

Money Facts

The *real* (plural *reais*) is Brazil's basic unit of currency. Its symbol is R$. One real is divided into 100 *centavos*. Paper money comes in values of 1, 2, 5, 10, 20, 50, and 100 reais. Coins come in values of 1, 5, 10, 25, and 50 centavos, and 1 real. In 2013, US$1 equaled R$1.97, and R$1 was equal to US$0.51. The U.S. dollar is the most widely accepted foreign currency in Brazil.

The front of Brazilian banknotes show the Head of the Republic—a symbolic image of a young woman with a crown of laurel leaves. On the reverse sides are various Brazilian animals such as the jaguar, macaw, and golden lion tamarin. The front of all coins show the Southern

Cross, a cluster of stars visible throughout Brazil. Various historic heroes appear on the coins' reverse side.

sugarcane, pineapples, oranges, orange juice concentrate, a twine-making fiber called sisal, and cashew apples, from which cashew nuts come. It ranks second in production of soybeans, papayas, tobacco, and Brazil nuts. Corn, cotton, wheat, rice, cocoa beans, beef, chicken, turkey, and pork are some other major Brazil farm products.

Brazil's agricultural success has come at a price. Farmers and ranchers have burned and cleared vast stretches of forestland in the Amazon Basin to make way for cropland and pastures. Illegal logging is rampant, too. The government has had some success in cracking down on forest clearing. By 2012, the forest was being destroyed at a slower rate than it had been in the previous twenty or more years. Still, destruction of the forest remains a major problem.

Manufacturing

For many years, Brazil's major factory goods were based on its farm products. Some of the top factory items were footwear, textiles and clothing, and processed foods and beverages. With such a huge supply of cattle for leather, Brazil could export its shoes and boots to countries around the world. Brazilian shoemakers even began making plastic shoes. Brazil's bountiful cotton crops made for a brisk trade in cotton cloth and clothes. Beef, sugar, and soy products sold well, and delicious fruits became juices and soft drinks.

These traditional products are still going strong. But the most valuable items rolling off Brazil's assembly lines now are heavy-duty industrial goods. Embraer, which is based in the state of São Paulo, is one of the world's largest producers of aircraft. In addition, most of the world's major car manufacturers, including Volkswagen, Toyota, and Ford, produce cars in Brazil. Other industrial products made in Brazil include motor vehicle parts, machinery for the oil industry, and construction materials such as iron and steel. Chemicals, cement, fertilizers, wood products, and mobile phones are also produced in Brazil.

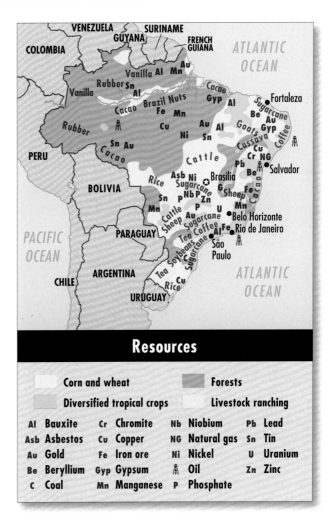

Resources

Corn and wheat		Forests
Diversified tropical crops		Livestock ranching

Al	Bauxite	Cr	Chromite	Nb	Niobium	Pb	Lead
Asb	Asbestos	Cu	Copper	NG	Natural gas	Sn	Tin
Au	Gold	Fe	Iron ore	Ni	Nickel	U	Uranium
Be	Beryllium	Gyp	Gypsum	Å	Oil	Zn	Zinc
C	Coal	Mn	Manganese	P	Phosphate		

What Brazil Grows, Makes, and Mines

AGRICULTURE (2011)

Sugarcane	715,143,562 metric tons
Soybeans	74,941,773 metric tons
Coffee beans	2,658,049 metric tons

MANUFACTURING (2008 EXPORTS)

Aircraft	US$5,495,000,000
Passenger cars	US$4,916,000,000
Motor vehicle parts	US$3,510,000,000

MINING

Petroleum (2011)	768,475,000 barrels
Iron ore (2009)	310,000,000 metric tons
Bauxite (2009)	28,200,000 metric tons

Mining

Gold and diamonds were Brazil's most valuable mining products in the 1700s. These precious resources enriched the Portuguese fortune hunters who swarmed in to mine them. Mining for gold, diamonds, and various gemstones is still going on in Brazil. However, other minerals have become more important to the economy. For example, Brazil is one of the world's largest producers of bauxite, graphite, iron ore, manganese, niobium, tantalum, and tin.

Petroleum is now Brazil's top mineral. Much of the country's oil drilling takes place in the waters offshore. Brazil exports some oil, but much of it remains in the country to be processed into fuels, lubricants, and other goods.

Brazil is also rich in iron ore. Iron is the main ingredient in steel, but pure iron is never found in nature. Instead, iron is extracted from iron ore, or rock that contains iron. The main type of iron ore mined in Brazil is called hematite. This mineral has a very high iron content, and Brazil produces more of it than any country in the world.

The Carajás Mine in northern Brazil is the largest iron mine in the world.

Brazil is the world's third-largest producer of bauxite, after Australia and China. Bauxite is the ore that contains aluminum. Bauxite is very valuable because there are so many aluminum products used in everyday life. They include cars and bikes, window and door frames, light poles, siding on houses, aluminum foil, pots and pans, and baseball bats.

Brazil provides around 90 percent of the world's supply of niobium. This element is added to steel to make it stronger. Niobium is also used in making jet engines, magnetic resonance imaging (MRI) scanners, coins, and jewelry. Other valuable Brazilian minerals are phosphates, platinum, uranium, copper, and coal.

A conveyor belt carries bauxite at a mining company in the Amazon rain forest.

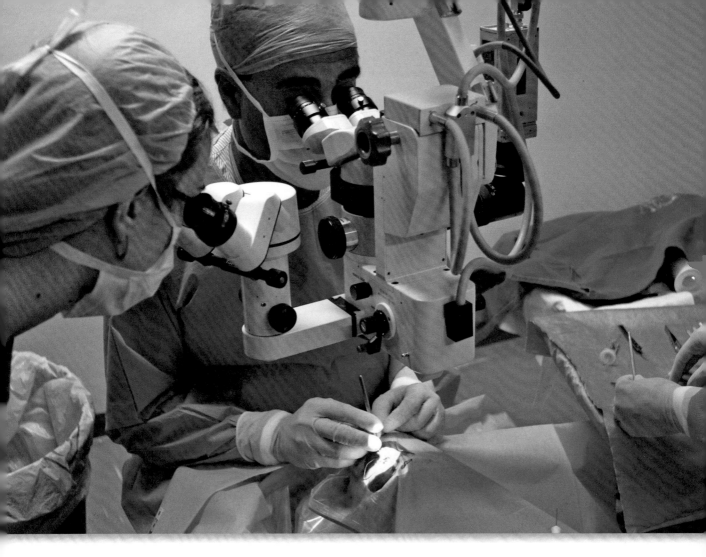

Services

Service industries play the largest role in Brazil's economy. Services account for about two-thirds of Brazil's GDP. People who work in service industries do not grow or make products. Instead, they do something for other people. Service providers include teachers, health care workers, government employees, salespeople, computer programmers, hairdressers, and people who repair everything from watches to trucks. About 60 percent of all Brazil's workers are employed in service industries.

Brazilian doctors perform surgery at a hospital in Recife.

The colorful, historic center of the city of Salvador is one of Brazil's many tourist attractions.

Tourism requires a large number of service workers. More than five million foreign tourists arrived in Brazil in 2011. Both local and foreign tourists rely on hotel and restaurant workers, tour guides, souvenir merchants, car and bus drivers, and other service providers. Foreign visitors also need to exchange their currency for the Brazilian real. Banking and other financial services make up a large portion of Brazil's service industry.

Communication

For every one hundred people in Brazil, there are 123 mobile phone subscriptions. That means that millions of Brazilians have more than one cell phone. Before mobile service arrived, someone who applied for landline service could wait years to get it! It's no wonder that cell phones are more popular than landlines.

An indigenous Brazilian works on his laptop at a conference in Rio de Janeiro.

Internet usage is also high in Brazil. In 2012, Brazil had about eighty-eight million Internet users, which was about 45 percent of the population. Brazilians spend an average of about twenty-seven hours a month online, but some experts predict that will increase to two hours a day by 2015. The government is in the process of bringing high-speed broadband Internet service to all public schools.

Brazilians publish more than five hundred daily print newspapers, reaching more than six million readers. The nation's top newspapers are Rio de Janeiro's *O Globo* and *O Dia* and São Paulo's *Folha de São Paulo* and *O Estado de São Paulo*. As in other countries, the Internet has had a big impact on newspaper circulation. Many Brazilian newspapers also publish an online version, making the future for print newspapers uncertain.

Ethanol: From Sugarcane to the Gas Tank

Brazil is the world leader in biofuels, or fuels made from plant materials. In Brazil, that plant is sugarcane. First sucrose is removed from the sugarcane to be made into ordinary sugar. Then the leftover waste fibers are processed into ethanol. People pump this fuel right into their cars' gas tanks. Ethanol fuel emits far less pollutants than gasoline. It is also much cheaper.

Most Brazilian carmakers build flex-fuel vehicles that run on a mix of gasoline and ethanol. By law, cars in Brazil must use an ethanol blend. Many drivers use no gasoline at all, instead filling their tanks with pure ethanol.

Transportation

Rio de Janeiro, São Paulo, Brasília, and several other large cities have rapid-transit train systems. Dozens of cities and towns also have tramways, or street-level railways. However, most Brazilians without cars use buses to get around town and to travel to other cities.

Brazil's longest highway, the BR-101, runs along the east coast. A little farther inland is the second-longest highway, BR-116. Both of these roads are heavily traveled because they pass through Rio de Janeiro and other big eastern cities. The Trans-Amazonian Highway is the next longest highway in the nation. It runs east and west, connecting the Amazon region with the rest of the country.

The Luz Station in São Paulo was completed in 1901. In the early twentieth century, the station was the main gateway into the city.

Much of the Trans-Amazonian Highway is unpaved and extremely difficult to maintain.

Though the Trans-Amazonian Highway was begun in the 1970s, it is still under construction. Much of this road has a dirt surface, and vehicles get stuck in the mud when heavy rains come. The highway has also contributed to deforestation of the Amazon region, since loggers' trucks are able to haul tons of timber out. On the other hand, the highway has enabled anthropologists, zoologists, and other scientists to travel to areas they could not reach before.

In many remote areas, people travel by horseback or on donkeys. Brazil has such a vast network of waterways that many villagers travel from town to town by boat on the rivers. This is also how tourists, scientists, and other explorers discover the wonders of Brazil's interior.

Horses are a common form of transportation in rural Brazil.

CHAPTER 7

Millions of Brazilians

J UST HOW MANY PEOPLE LIVE IN BRAZIL? EXACT population figures are hard to pin down. Pockets of people are overlooked, some cannot be reached, and uncounted babies are born every day. Brazil's 2010 census counted 190.8 million people. In 2012, the government updated that figure to 193.9 million. However, other estimates put the 2012 population as high as 206 million. Brazil is not only the world's fifth-largest country in land area. It also has the fifth-largest population. The only countries with more residents are China, India, the United States, and Indonesia.

Most Brazilians live near the Atlantic coast. That's where they find the best farmland, the largest industrial cities, and the most jobs. About four-fifths of all Brazilians live within 200 miles (300 km) of the coast. Away from the coastal areas, the population gradually thins out. Southeastern Brazil is the most densely populated region. On the other extreme, people are spread out very thinly in the Amazon region. Only about 13 percent of the population lives there.

Opposite: **Ipanema Beach in Rio de Janeiro is often packed with people.**

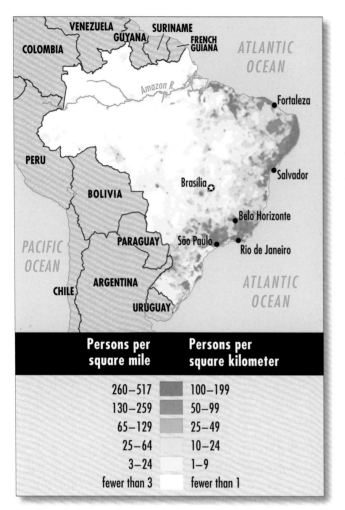

Persons per square mile		Persons per square kilometer
260–517		100–199
130–259		50–99
65–129		25–49
25–64		10–24
3–24		1–9
fewer than 3		fewer than 1

São Paulo, Brazil's largest city, is the seventh-largest city in the world. The city itself had a 2012 population of 11,376,685. Almost 20 million people lived in São Paulo's metropolitan area, which includes the surrounding suburbs. Brazil's next-largest cities are Rio de Janeiro, on the southeast coast; Salvador, on the northeast coast; Brasília, in the interior; and Fortaleza, another northeastern coastal city.

Pathways to Brazil

Strains of European, African, and Indian ancestry run through the people of Brazil. Indigenous people were the only residents for thousands of years. Then in the 1500s, Portuguese settlers swept in. Eventually they brought in almost four million Africans as slaves. Other waves of newcomers sailed into Brazil's harbors, many looking for a new start in a new land.

The mid-1800s saw an influx of Germans, who settled and farmed in the south. The late 1800s brought many Italian immigrants. Some settled in the mountainous regions, while others worked on the coffee plantations in São Paulo state. More immigrants came from Portugal and Spain. Japanese people began arriving in the early 1900s to work on the cof-

Population of Major Cities (2012 est.)

São Paulo	11,376,685
Rio de Janeiro	6,390,290
Salvador	2,710,965
Brasília	2,645,532
Fortaleza	2,500,194

fee farms. Heavy Japanese immigration continued throughout the twentieth century. Today, Brazil has the largest Japanese population outside of Japan.

After World War I (1914–1918), political conditions in their home countries drove people from many lands to Brazil. They included Europeans from Poland, Russia, and Romania, as well as Middle Eastern people from Syria and Lebanon. Brazil's booming factories needed more workers in the 1950s, so laborers came from Spain, Italy, and Greece. In the late 1900s and early 2000s, new immigrants included people from Angola, Korea, China, and the neighboring countries of Bolivia and Argentina. Still, Portuguese people were the foreigners with the earliest and longest foothold in the country. That's why Portuguese is Brazil's national language.

Workers make snacks at a food stall in São Paulo. About half of Japanese Brazilians live in São Paulo state.

Ethnicity in Brazil (2010)

White	47.7%
Brown	43.1%
Black	7.6%
East Asian	1.1%
Indigenous	0.4%

Brazilian children playing at the beach

Identifying Ethnic Roots

Brazil's census asks people to name their skin color. This identifies how people think of themselves. It provides a snapshot of people's cultural identity, rather than a scientific analysis of their ethnic makeup. Many Brazilians say that they do not pay much attention to ethnic background. Various ethnic groups in Brazil mixed for five hundred years, and most Brazilians have some mixture in their background.

Almost 48 percent of Brazilians classify themselves as white, with largely European ancestry. They live throughout the country, but mainly in the south and southeast. Another 43 percent call themselves *pardo*, which translates as "brown." They include people of mixed ancestry. The greatest number of people who identify as brown live in the north and northeast. Black Brazilians, or Afro-Brazilians, make up 7.6 percent of the population. Most live in northeastern Brazil, where African slavery was predominant. Just over 1 percent of Brazilians claim East Asian ancestry, with most having origins in Japan. Most Asian Brazilians live in the south. Finally, indigenous people, or Indians, make up only 0.4 percent. Most of them live in the vast Amazon region. Many experts believe that indigenous people and Black Brazilians are undercounted.

Many black Brazilians live in Bahia state of northeastern Brazil.

A Terena man takes part in a ceremony at a meeting in Rio de Janeiro. The Terena are among the largest of the approximately two hundred indigenous groups in Brazil today.

Indigenous Peoples

Before the Portuguese arrived in what is now Brazil, an estimated two million to five million Indians lived there. They were organized into tribal groups, and their traditional way of life involved hunting forest animals, fishing, gathering plants, and farming. Invasions of farmers, cattle ranchers, loggers, rubber tappers, and miners uprooted the Indians from their lands. Diseases, wars, and outright killings cut their numbers dramatically. Today, Brazil is home to about 818,000 indigenous people. In recent decades, this number has been growing.

Over the years, many Indians left their traditional territories, adopted Western clothes and lifestyles, and took jobs in cities and towns. Many married outside their tribal groups. Millions of Brazilians today have some Indian ancestry.

By the 1960s, the government began to realize that the Indians needed protection. In 1961, it created Xingu National Park in Mato Grosso state. This was the first of several reserves set up to protect Indians and their traditional way of life. In 1967, the government established Fundação Nacional do Índio (FUNAI; National Indian Foundation) to oversee Indian affairs. Since then, laws have been passed to protect Indians and their territories. Nevertheless, loggers, miners, and ranchers continue their invasions. They penetrate deep into traditional lands, opening up roads, burning vast swaths of forestland, and murdering inhabitants.

Now there are more than 650 indigenous reserves in the Amazon region, covering almost 13 percent of the country. About 240 tribal groups remain today, but only a few of them live completely traditional lives. The largest groups are the Yanomami on the Brazil-Venezuela border and the Guaraní in southern Mato Grosso state. Other large tribes include the Macuxi of northern Brazil's Roraima state and the Kayapó of Pará and Mato Grosso states. A small number of Indians have never had contact with

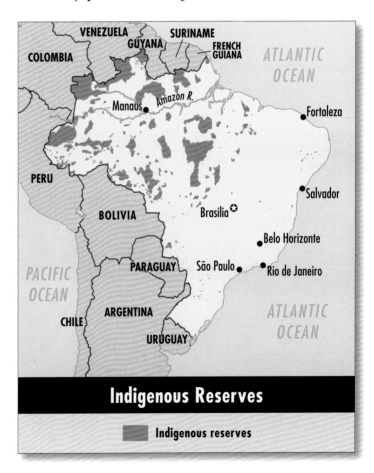

Indigenous Reserves

Indigenous reserves

Running for Their Lives

"Many Awá are still uncontacted, and they are running for their lives." This statement comes from Survival International, an organization that defends indigenous peoples of the world.

The Awá people live in the rain forests of Maranhão state, in northeastern Brazil. They are considered the most endangered tribe in the Amazon region. Only around 300 Awá people are still alive, and about 100 of them have had no contact with outsiders.

People are pouring into traditional Awá territory. They set up illegal settlements, clear land for cattle ranches, and take their chainsaws to valuable trees. Giant trucks piled high with huge tree trunks go rumbling out. Observers of FUNAI, the National Indian Foundation, watch them but can do nothing. The truck drivers are armed.

The destruction began in the 1980s, when a railway was built to haul iron ore to the coast. It cut right through Awá land. Roads followed the railway, bringing settlers and loggers. Since then, one-third of the forest in Awá territory has been destroyed.

Hired gunmen are on patrol to clear the way for land-grabbers. One Awá man described an invasion by ranchers: "I hid in the forest and escaped from the white people," he said. "They killed my mother, my brothers and sisters and my wife."

Another Awá man expressed the fears of all his hunter-gatherer tribe: "Monkeys, peccaries, tapir, they are all running away. I don't know how we are going to eat—everything is being destroyed. . . . This land is mine, it is ours. . . . Everything is dying. We are all going to go hungry, the children will be hungry, my daughter will be hungry, and I'll be hungry too." If such conditions continue, the Awá will become extinct.

Speaking Portuguese

Oi.	Hello.
Como vai?	How are you?
Muito bem. E você?	Very well. And you?
Como se chama?	What's your name?
Meu nome é . . .	My name is . . .
Muito obrigado.	Thank you very much.
De nada.	You're welcome.
Não entendi.	I don't understand.
Como se diz . . . em português?	How do you say . . . in Portuguese?
Bom dia.	Good morning.
Boa tarde.	Good afternoon/evening.
Boa noite.	Good night.
Tchau.	Good-bye.

outsiders. FUNAI estimates that as many as seventy uncontacted groups live in the Amazon rain forest today.

Language

Portuguese is the official language in Brazil, and almost everyone in the country speaks it. Over the centuries, Brazilian Portuguese has developed differently from European Portuguese. People from Brazil and Portugal can understand one another, but they have different accents and use some different words. It is much like the difference between American English and British English.

About 180 indigenous languages are spoken in Brazil. The most prominent of these include Guaraní, Nheengatu, Tucano, and Apalaí. In southern Brazil, Italian, German, Arabic, and Mandarin Chinese are spoken in some communities where many immigrants settled.

CHAPTER 8

Spiritual Life

BRAZILIANS EXPRESS THEIR SPIRITUALITY IN MANY ways. Religious feast days may find hundreds of people in solemn procession behind a statue. New Year's Eve may find white-robed people casting flowers into the sea. A lighted candle may invoke the blessings of a saint or a mythical being. Like many aspects of Brazilian culture, religious practices reflect Brazil's cultural mix. Many people take part in the devotions and ceremonies of more than one religion.

Roman Catholicism

Roman Catholicism arrived in Brazil with Portuguese settlers, and Catholic missionaries continued to spread the faith. The tall steeples of Catholic churches rise high over every city and town. Many ornate churches were gifts of wealthy colonists who donated money to build houses of worship. Today, about two-thirds of all Brazilians belong to the Catholic faith. In fact, more Catholics live in Brazil than in any other country in the world. Although most Brazilians claim to be Catholic, many are not active members who attend services regularly.

Religions in Brazil (2010)	
Roman Catholic	64.6%
Evangelical Protestant	22.2%
No religion	8.0%
Other religions	5.2%

Other Faiths

Many Brazilians belong to non-Catholic Christian faiths. They include Anglicans, as well as Protestants such as Lutherans, Methodists, Baptists, and Presbyterians. Protestant Pentecostal, fundamentalist, and evangelical groups have gained many new members since the 1990s. Brazil's Japanese people traditionally practice Shinto or Buddhism. Members of the Lebanese and Syrian communities follow Islam or Maronite Catholicism. Jehovah's Witness, Judaism, Baha'ism, and Mormonism are among Brazil's other minority religions.

A man takes part in a Buddhist ceremony in São Paulo. Brazil has the largest Buddhist population in South America.

Evangelicals and Charismatics

Evangelicals are the fastest-growing religious group in the country. Only about 6.6 percent of Brazilians claimed to be evangelicals in 1980. By 2010, evangelical groups made up 22.2 percent of the population. Evangelical worship services are especially popular. They often include enthusiastic singing and faith healing. Evangelical churches also emphasize a personal relationship with God. Their teachings are very conservative, and they promote a clean, moral lifestyle. In a country riddled with corruption, drug problems, and other social ills, many find this appealing.

Every year Brazilian evangelical Christians hold a huge march in São Paulo. In 2012, more than a million people attended.

Catholics in Brazil are most likely to go to church on religious holidays and feast days.

Over the years, many Catholics joined evangelical churches. For them, evangelical services provided a more dynamic religious experience than they had had in Catholic churches. Still, studies show that the biggest threat to Brazil's traditional faith is indifference. By the twenty-first century, more Brazilians than ever were abandoning religion altogether. They simply were not interested. According to Brazil's 2010 census, fifteen million Brazilians declared they had no religion. Between 2000 and 2010, Catholic adherents dropped from 73.6 percent to 64.6 percent.

With a declining membership, Catholic leaders looked for ways to keep Catholicism vital and meaningful. The Catholic Charismatic Renewal (CCR) movement led the way. Charismatic priests adopted evangelical methods, infusing their services with rousing music, dance, and audience participation. This approach is attracting more followers, both young and old, who enjoy a lively, happy religious experience. In 2013, CCR members were involved in organizing World Youth Day in Rio de Janeiro. This event brought together many thousands of young, enthusiastic Catholics from around the world.

Religious Feast Days and Festivals

Brazilians celebrate many religious holidays and saints' feast days throughout the year. Many of these celebrations evolved from Portuguese feasts of colonial times, taking on local Brazilian customs along the way. Most festivals include a mass, the major Catholic worship service, followed by a procession.

The Pop-Star Priest

Brazil's most famous Catholic priest is Father Marcelo Rossi, based in Santo Amaro in São Paulo state. His services typically attract thousands of worshippers, and he issues millions of best-selling CDs, DVDs, and books. Rossi is often called the pop-star priest because he includes rock music at his masses and his songs have been nominated for Latin Grammys. His Mother of God sanctuary, under construction in 2013, will hold twenty thousand people, with room outside for eighty thousand more to watch services on huge video screens. Rossi sees a lack of interest as the Catholic Church's biggest threat, and he hopes to foster heartfelt devotion among his followers. "My calling is to spark among Brazilians the love for the Church, the Eucharist and Mary. "

On New Year's Day in Salvador, the faithful honor Bom Jesus dos Navegantes, or Good Jesus of Seafarers. The day begins with a mass in the city's cathedral. Then the statue of Bom Jesus is taken from the church down to the harbor. From there, it is placed on a special boat, followed by hundreds of small boats decorated with flags and streamers. The four-hour waterborne procession glides across to the beach of Boa Viagem. Thousands of people line the shore to watch the event. According to tradition, sailors who take part in this devotion will be safe from drowning.

Sailors row a boat carrying the image of Bom Jesus during the procession of Bom Jesus dos Navegantes in Salvador.

The Feast of the Divine Holy Spirit takes place in May or June. Festivities can last for days, and each town has its own way of celebrating. In Paraty, south of Rio de Janeiro, townspeople parade through the streets for nine days carrying red flags to the church. A man is crowned as emperor, a boy is crowned as the prince, and children get bags of sweets. Pirenópolis, in Goiás state, holds the *cavalhadas*, a horseback reenactment of a medieval European battle between Christians and Muslims.

June Festivals celebrate the feast days of Saint Anthony (June 13), Saint John (June 24), and Saint Peter (June 29). Some cities observe the festivals for the whole month. The northeastern cities of Caruaru and Campina Grande claim to have the grandest festival of all.

The fifteen-day festival of Círio de Nazaré is one of the largest celebrations in the world. It is held in Belém to honor the Virgin Mary, Jesus's mother. As the Virgin of Nazaré, she is the patron saint of Pará state. More than a million pilgrims take part in the climax of the festival on the second Sunday of October. They follow an image of the Virgin of Nazaré through the streets of Belém.

Many Brazilians enjoy Afro-Brazilian religious celebrations. The best known is the Iemanjá Festival, honoring the mother goddess of the sea. On New Year's Eve in Rio de Janeiro, participants dressed in white gather on Copacabana Beach and toss flowers into the sea. Thousands of people in Salvador celebrate the same festival on February 2, setting flowers and other offerings afloat in little boats.

A Candomblé priestess performs a ritual on a beach in Rio de Janeiro.

Candomblé and Umbanda

Brazil's ethnic mix spills over into its spiritual life. The country became a fertile ground for syncretic religions, or those with a blend of belief systems. Among those religions, the most widely practiced are Candomblé and Umbanda. Also called Afro-Brazilian religions, both are mixtures of African and Catholic traditions.

Candomblé mixes African folk beliefs with Catholic symbols. It is prevalent in Bahia state, where it began among West African people imported as slaves. They brought their ancient rituals with them, including the worship of several *orixás*, or deities. Forced to accept Catholicism, the enslaved Africans transformed their orixás into Catholic versions. Oxalá, the god of fertility and harvests, was merged with Jesus. Iemanjá, the sea goddess and mother of all orixás, became Mary, the mother of Jesus. Ogum, the god of war, became Saint George; Xangô, the god of thunder and fire, became Saint Jerome, and so on. Images of orixás were often hidden inside the statues of Catholic saints. The saints' images eventually became a part of Candomblé worship.

Candomblé ceremonies often take place at night. Participants arrange flowers, candles, and ritual ornaments around the ceremonial site. Accompanied by rhythmic drumbeats, they chant and dance, calling upon the orixás. Some members, possessed by the deities, fall into a trance. Christian

On February 2, Candomblé followers carry flowers and other gifts for Iemanjá, the goddess of the sea, to her shrine in Salvador.

Indian Spirituality

Each of Brazil's indigenous groups has its own spiritual beliefs and practices. Reverence for the natural world is common to them all. According to a Yanomami shaman, or spiritual leader, "Omama, our creator, made us think and talk with the soul of the forest." Omama gave the forest to the Yanomami as their world for all time. According to the Yanomami, spirits inhabit every animal, stone, tree, river, cloud, and mountain. Shamans connect with the spirits to heal the sick, interpret dreams, predict the weather, and drive off evil.

Among the Guaraní, each village has its spiritual leader and an opy, a house for prayer and rituals. Prayers take the form of songs, dances, and speeches, appealing for good weather, bountiful harvests, family blessings, and so on. The year's major event is the Nheemongarai ceremony. Traditional crops are gathered in the opy and blessed, and babies born over the previous year are given their names.

For the Kayapó, the village is the center of their world. They believe that potentially dangerous spirits occupy the forest outside the village, and these spirits must be appeased with chants and rituals. For example, after the hunt, men must sing to the dead animal's spirit so it will stay in the forest. Shamans contact the spirits of nature to find out their names and songs. A name from nature is then given in a child's naming ceremony, during which villagers sing and dance through the night.

churches have tried to discourage Candomblé, but without much success. Brazilian laws to control Candomblé were lifted in the 1970s, and its popularity soared.

Umbanda originated in Rio de Janeiro in the early 1900s. It combines elements of Candomblé, Catholicism, and Spiritism, a belief in contacting the spirit world. Umbandists worship one supreme creator. They also honor African spirits, as in Candomblé, and merge these spirits with Catholic saints. Umbandists claim to rely on white magic (good magic), in contrast to the dark tone of Candomblé. They make offerings of candles and food to their spirit protectors, who may be

Catholic saints, African deities, or historical heroes. Many use magic potions to heal illness or attract love.

Many other Afro-Brazilian religions are offshoots of Candomblé and Umbanda. Most Brazilians who practice an Afro-Brazilian or indigenous religion also practice Catholicism or evangelical Christianity.

Creatures of Folklore

Brazilian folklore is peppered with mythical creatures that help people or scare them. Most are creatures of Indian lore that seeped into the wider Brazilian culture.

An altar in an Umbanda house of worship. Some Brazilians have been hostile toward the practice of the Umbanda religion.

The *caipora* of the Tupi-Guaraní is a dark, hairy, cigar-smoking creature that rides through the forest on a wild boar. The caipora myth sometimes blends with the tale of another forest creature, the *curupira*. This is a redheaded, boyish creature with feet pointing backward. He protects the forest because his backward footprints cause hunters and loggers to become confused and lost. In São Paulo state, the curupira is the symbolic protector of the forest and its creatures.

The *cobra grande* (large serpent) of the Amazon waterways is said to shift into different shapes to frighten fishermen. In the 1800s, Brazilians merged this water snake with the

Dancers perform in a contest during the festival of St. John in Belo Horizonte.

European myth of the siren, a beautiful half-woman–half-fish creature who lured sailors to their death. The result was the mother of waters, with the Tupi name of Iara. Cultures merged yet again, with Iara being identified with the Afro-Brazilian deity Iemanjá, the sea goddess.

The *boto* is the pink dolphin of the Amazon region. In June, during the festival of Saint John, the boto is said to change into a handsome man and come to the festive dances. Because his dolphin nostrils are still on top of his head, he leaves his hat on. Then he charms some innocent young lady and lures her back to his underwater abode. By tradition, men at this festival are asked to remove their hats to prove they are not the boto in disguise.

The mischievous little *saci*, or *saci-pererê*, haunts the south-central plateaus. This one-legged boy wears a magical red cap and smokes a pipe. He makes food burn, slams doors, turns cattle loose, and frightens people traveling alone in the forest. Anyone who can get hold of the saci's hat will have a wish come true.

The *negrinho do pastoreio* (little black shepherd) is a legend of southern Brazil's ranching country. The young shepherd fell asleep, and his herd wandered away. The cruel ranch boss punished the boy severely and left him in an anthill to be eaten up. Blessed by the Virgin Mary, the boy came back to ride forever through the land on a swift bay horse. Whoever loses something should light a candle in the negrinho's honor, and he will help find it. This tale arose among the region's black slaves. It was passed along by word of mouth and took on many versions in poetry and prose.

CHAPTER 9

Creative Culture

BRAZILIAN CULTURE IS A VIBRANT MIX OF PORTUGUESE, indigenous, and African influences. These three strains can be seen in Brazilians' many forms of self-expression and creativity. Above all, the sheer joy of living is displayed through various forms of artistic expression.

Opposite: **Carnival dancers dress in spectacular, colorful costumes.**

The Samba and Carnival

The samba is Brazil's most spectacular dance. Like much Brazilian music, the samba began with African music and dance rhythms. Many different samba styles developed as Portuguese and pop music mixed with the African beat. Foreigners fell in love with the samba in the 1930s, and ballroom dancers scrambled to learn it.

No one thinks of samba without thinking of Carnival. This is the biggest party of the year in Brazil. Carnival has the same spiritual roots as the Mardi Gras festival in other parts of the world. It takes place in February or March, before Ash

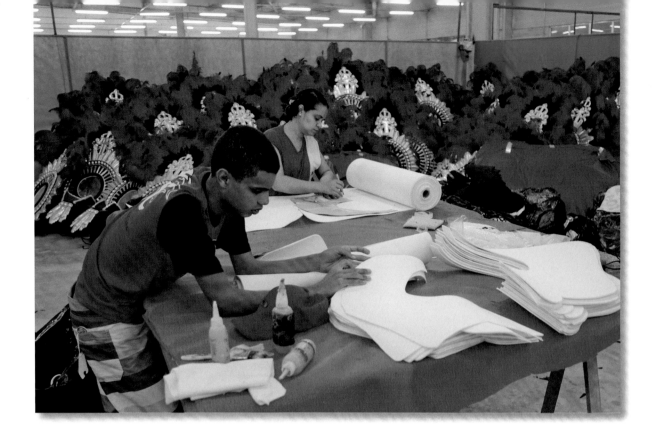

It often takes months for samba schools to make all their costumes for Carnival.

Wednesday ushers in the somber season of Lent. Lent is the time leading up to Easter when Christians lead quiet, sober lives and meditate on Jesus's suffering and death. So Carnival traditionally is a time to cut loose and have fun.

In Rio de Janeiro, some *sambistas* (samba dancers) spend all year getting ready for the Carnival parade. Each samba school designs its dance moves, costumes, and float for the event. Glittery sequins, extravagant feathers, sparkling jewels, and shimmering materials adorn both dancers and floats. Sambistas parade down the Sambadrome, a stretch of road lined with stadium seats and tens of thousands of cheering fans. Competition is fierce, as each school competes for the grand prize. Rio's samba parade is the most famous, but several other cities have their own versions.

Music

Heitor Villa-Lobos was a classical music composer of the early 1900s. Most other composers of the time were writing in a European style. But Villa-Lobos's music was based on Portuguese, Indian, and African folk tunes and rhythms. One of his best-known pieces is the *Bachianas Brasileiras*. Classical music of all kinds is popular in Brazil, and thousands of people attend free outdoor classical concerts in the larger cities.

In the 1950s, João Gilberto and Antônio Carlos Jobim created the bossa nova music style. This fusion of samba and jazz soon migrated to the United States and Europe. Jobim's hit song "The Girl from Ipanema" became a classic of the 1960s.

Antônio Carlos Jobim helped create bossa nova, a quiet and intimate type of Brazilian music.

Aleijadinho and His Sculptures

Antônio Francisco Lisboa (ca. 1738–1814) is one of Brazil's most famous sculptors and architects. Born in Ouro Preto, Lisboa was the son of a Portuguese carpenter and an enslaved African. He learned the basics of sculpture and architecture from his father. When he was around thirty years old, his hands began to become deformed, possibly because of a devastating disease called leprosy. Then people began to call him Aleijadinho, "Little Cripple."

Embarrassed by his disability, Aleijadinho tried to stay out of the public eye. Nevertheless, he kept on working. He had helpers strap a hammer and chisel to his arms so he could sculpt figures in wood and stone. As his feet deteriorated, he had pads strapped to his knees for climbing ladders.

Aleijadinho's most famous work is at the Sanctuary of Bom Jesus do Congonhas in Minas Gerais, south of Belo Horizonte. Statues of twelve Biblical figures carved in soapstone decorate the outdoor courtyard. Around the church are seven chapels illustrating the Stations of the Cross, the stages leading up to Jesus's crucifixion. In these chapels, Aleijadinho carved more than sixty multicolored wooden figures, each showing highly expressive emotions.

Singer-songwriter-guitarist Milton Nascimento combines folk music, jazz, rock, bossa nova, and classical styles. His music has won worldwide appeal and earned several Grammy Award nominations.

Art and Architecture

Brazil's most beloved sculptor is Antônio Francisco Lisboa. He is commonly known as Aleijadinho, or "Little Cripple," because of his deformed hands. Aleijadinho's work adorns many ornate colonial churches in Minas Gerais.

In the 1800s, most Brazilian artists painted in the formal style of European artists. Cândido Portinari changed that trend in the twentieth century. Using vivid colors and stark lines, he portrayed scenes of Brazilians in everyday life.

Teatro Amazonas

Rubber barons used their wealth to build the fabulous Teatro Amazonas, or Amazon Theater. It stands in Manaus, at the edge of the Amazon rain forest. Construction began in 1884 and took until 1896 to complete. This ornate opera house features marble and chandeliers from Italy, roof tiles from France, and cast iron from Scotland. Covering the dome are thirty-six thousand ceramic tiles in the colors of the Brazilian flag. Many international opera stars sang there in its early days. When Brazil's rubber market crashed in the early 1900s, the rubber barons left and the theater closed down. Today it has been restored, and some of Europe's finest musicians perform there.

Portinari chose subjects such as laborers, poor families, and people grieving for their dead. He also painted huge murals, or wall-sized paintings. Some of them adorn the Library of Congress in Washington, D.C., and the United Nations building in New York City, New York.

Architect Oscar Niemeyer's buildings are known for their spacious interiors, abstract shapes, and dramatic curves. His buildings can be found in cities all over the world. Niemeyer's most famous works are the government buildings and cathedral in Brasília. He also took part in designing the United Nations headquarters.

Oscar Niemeyer helped design the UN Building in the International Style of architecture. This style uses simple rectangular shapes stripped of decoration.

Literature

Early Brazilian writers had a colonial point of view. They wrote of voyages to Brazil, encounters with Indians, activities of the missionaries, or uprisings against colonial rule. In the 1830s, the poet Gonçalves de Magalhães introduced romanticism to the country. This literary style featured deep emotions, the beauties of nature, a sense of being Brazilian, and the use of everyday spoken language instead of stiff, formal language. By this time, Brazilians were becoming more aware of their unique identity and their Indian ancestry. With this point of view, many writers of the time focused on Indian themes. Well-known examples are José de Alencar's novels *Iracema* and *The Guarani*, which was made into an opera.

Romanticism gave way to realism in the late 1800s. Writers began to portray the harsh realities of class conflict. Joaquim Maria Machado de Assis, the grandson of freed slaves, made fun of Rio's high society in *Epitaph of a Small Winner*. His *Dom Casmurro* (Sir Frown), about a bitter, jealous husband, became popular all over the world. Euclides da Cunha's *Os Sertões* (*Rebellion in the Backlands*) delves into a peasant revolt against wealthy landowners.

Joaquim Maria Machado de Assis is considered one of Brazil's greatest writers. He is renowned for his dark but funny stories.

The novels of Jorge Amado are widely read around the world. His work has been translated into forty-nine languages.

Jorge Amado is Brazil's most popular modern novelist. He wrote about the plight of poor urban people in his native Bahia in *Gabriela, Clove and Cinnamon* and other novels. *Gabriela, Clove and Cinnamon* was made into a movie and a TV series, as was Amado's novel *Dona Flor and Her Two Husbands*. Amado's novels have been translated into dozens of languages. Although he died in 2001, his work continues to reflect Brazil's social conditions in a sympathetic and joyful way.

Capoeira

Capoeira can be called a martial art, a dance, a game, gymnastics, or all of these. It relies on tricky, deceptive moves. Two *capoeiristas* may battle each other alone in a martial arts competition. But in a community setting, spectators begin by forming a circle called the *roda*. They sing and clap to the rhythm of a drum, tambourine, and stringed instrument. Then the two capoeiristas face off in the center of the circle, challenging each other with energetic but graceful kicks and acrobatic moves.

Brazil's enslaved Africans developed capoeira to defend themselves against Portuguese colonists. After slavery was abolished, capoeira was outlawed. The practice continued, though. Practitioners claimed it was just a dance. By the mid-twentieth century, capoeira was starting to be considered a national sport. Capoeira schools are found throughout Brazil, as well as in the United States and Europe.

Capoeira includes graceful tumbling and kicking that looks like a martial art.

Futebol!

Brazilians are wild about *futebol*, also known as soccer. It is the national sport. Any patch of dirt is likely to turn into a soccer field at a moment's notice. There are thousands of soccer teams around the country. Several hundred teams belong to the Brazilian Football League. They compete in state and national championships. Cities, towns, schools, businesses, and neighborhoods all have soccer teams, too. Each team has its cheering pack of loyal fans.

Brazil's national team is the most successful team in the history of the World Cup, international soccer's preeminent tournament. As of 2012, the team has won the World Cup five

Brazilian girls play soccer on a beach. Brazil has the most successful women's national soccer team in South America.

times: in 1958, 1962, 1970, 1994, and 2002. The whole nation was thrilled when Brazil was chosen to host the 2014 World Cup.

Brazil has produced many international soccer stars. The most famous of them all is Pelé, a legend of the 1960s. He played in four World Cups and is the only player to win three World Cups. In the early 2000s, one leading soccer star was Ronaldo Luis Nazário de Lima—best known as simply Ronaldo. Today, the country's top star is Neymar da Silva Santos Júnior, better known as Neymar.

Pelé kicks a ball over his head during a soccer game in 1968. He is generally considered the greatest soccer player of all time.

Other Sports

Brazilians enjoy many other sports besides soccer. Volleyball is Brazil's second most popular sport. The national volleyball teams—both men's and women's—have brought home dozens of medals from the Olympics, the Volleyball World Cup, and the Volleyball Club World Championships.

Neymar

In recent years, nobody has created more excitement on the soccer fields of Brazil than Neymar da Silva Santos Júnior. Everyone calls him simply Neymar. He usually plays forward and is known for his explosive energy and creativity on the field. Neymar, who was born in 1992, showed his extraordinary skill very early in life. At age eleven, he began playing on the youth team of the Santos club in São Paulo. He began playing with the Santos professional team, one of the top teams in Brazil, when he was just seventeen years old. By the time he was nineteen, he had been named the South American soccer player of the year in a poll of journalists. Today, he is considered one of the greatest players in the world.

With its miles of sandy beaches, Brazil is also a natural spot for beach volleyball. Players were ecstatic when beach volleyball became an official Olympic sport in 1996. Since then, Brazil's men and women volleyball athletes have earned gold or silver medals in every event.

Brazil's Fernanda Rodrigues reaches for the ball during a volleyball match at the 2012 Olympics. Brazil's women's volleyball team won the gold medal.

All together, Brazilian athletes have won more than one hundred Olympic medals. Their top medal-winning sports are volleyball, sailing, and judo. Excitement spread nationwide when Rio de Janeiro won its bid to host the 2016 Summer Olympic Games.

Other popular sports in Brazil are rugby, basketball, skateboarding, mixed martial arts, and auto racing. Brazilian race car driver Emerson Fittipaldi won the Formula One World Championship in 1972 and 1974. In 1972, at just age twenty-five, he was the youngest winner ever of the Formula One race. Fittipaldi won the Indianapolis 500 twice, in 1989 and 1993. Another top Brazilian race car driver, Ayrton Senna, won three Formula One World Championships. He was killed in a race in 1994. Brazil holds its own championship race, the Brazilian Grand Prix, in São Paulo every year.

Maracanã Stadium

Maracanã Stadium in Rio de Janeiro is one of the largest stadiums in the world. It holds about eighty-two thousand people. Maracanã was built for the 1950 World Cup soccer championships. It was renovated to prepare for two blockbuster events: the 2014 World Cup and the 2016 Summer Olympics. Maracanã hosts more than sporting events. Frank Sinatra, Tina Turner, the Rolling Stones, Madonna, Paul McCartney, and the Back Street Boys all performed there. When Pope John Paul II, the then leader of the Roman Catholic Church, visited Brazil in 1980, he said a mass at Maracanã.

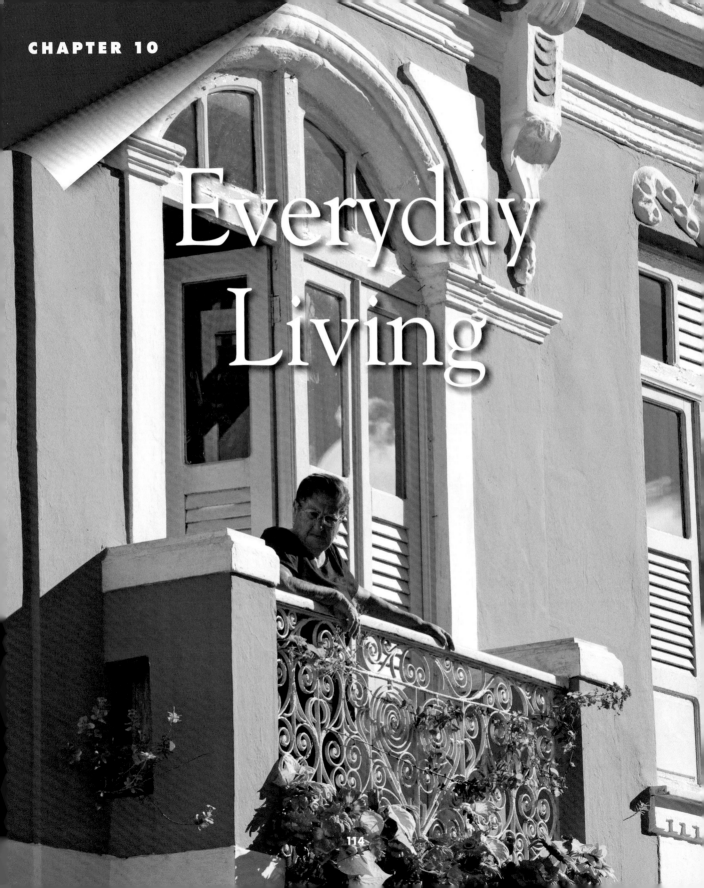

CHAPTER 10

Everyday Living

LIFE IN BRAZIL'S BIG CITIES IS MUCH LIKE LIFE IN North America's urban areas. Tall buildings line the busy streets, and sidewalks are jammed with pedestrians. Many cities also have an older district with narrow lanes and historic buildings.

Some city residents live in modern apartment buildings, while others have homes in the suburbs. Most middle-class Brazilians own a car. But with or without a car, the bus is the most practical transportation for many people. Morning rush hour finds workers scurrying to their jobs in office buildings and stores. They may meet friends after work at a café or dance club before heading home. After dinner, people like to watch *telenovelas*, Brazil's wildly popular prime-time soap operas. Weekends are the time to go shopping at a mall, have a barbecue, or watch a soccer game.

Favelas

Living conditions in favelas have long been a major problem in Brazil. Favelas are settlements on the outskirts of town where poor people live. Life there can be harsh, and crime,

Opposite: **Many Brazilian towns feature colorful buildings from colonial times.**

gang activity, and drug wars are rampant. Most favelas were established during the 1970s, when thousands of rural people moved to the cities to find work. They couldn't afford apartments, so they built shacks of cardboard and tin.

Brazil has more than six thousand favelas. They are home to more than eleven million people, or about 6 percent of the population. Almost half the favelas are in the southeast, because that's where the biggest cities are. Favelas are found in Rio de Janeiro, São Paulo, Salvador, Recife, Olinda, Brasília, and many other cities.

Rocinha, in Rio de Janeiro, is one of the nation's largest favelas. It is home to an estimated 120,000 people.

National Holidays

New Year's Day	January 1
Carnival	February or early March
Good Friday	March or April
Tiradentes Day	April 21
Labor Day	May 1
Corpus Christi	May or June
Independence Day	September 7
Our Lady of Aparecida	October 12
All Souls' Day	November 2
Day of the Republic	November 15
Black Consciousness Day	November 20
Christmas Day	December 25

The government has worked to improve life in the favelas, bringing sanitation, running water, electricity, and garbage service to many of them. Special police units work to bring down the criminal activity. Tourists are even encouraged to visit favelas to see what dynamic communities they have become. Rocinha, in Rio, is the country's largest favela, with more than one hundred thousand residents. It has become a well-developed neighborhood, with brick houses, schools, libraries, banks, and other businesses.

Rural Life

Life in the rural countryside is much different from city life. Millions of rural people live in one- or two-room homes built of stones, wood, or adobe, a mixture of mud and straw. Some rural residents live by subsistence farming, scratching out crops on their dusty land. Some work in factories or on ranches or plantations. They work long hours for low wages. Other

Wedding Traditions

Most Brazilian weddings take place in a church, followed by a party in a hall or banquet room. Some customs are different from those in the United States and Canada, though.

For the wedding party, the bride and groom do not choose their attendants separately. Instead, they choose three couples as their *padrinhos* (godfathers) and *madrinhos* (godmothers). Padrinhos wear a little Brazilian flag instead of a flower.

Each table at the reception is named for a Brazilian city, such as São Paulo, Rio de Janeiro, and Salvador. Guests receive cookies called *casadinhos* or *bem casados* (well married) as a wedding favor. Casadinhos consist of two cookies stuck together with honey, jam, cream, or fudge. They symbolize the bride and groom sweetly joined together in a happy life.

At one point, a padrinho takes out a pair of large scissors and invites guests to chop off pieces of the groom's tie. After dinner, everyone dances to pagode music, a joyful version of samba. Festivities go on into the night, ending only when all the food is gone!

people get only seasonal work during harvest times. Countless rural Brazilians own no land, while wealthy landowners possess millions of acres of vacant land. In the 1980s, some rural workers organized the Landless Workers' Movement, which works to change land ownership laws.

Caiçaras and *caboclos* are people of mixed Indian and Portuguese ancestry. Many are descended from marriages between Portuguese and Indians that took place during the rubber boom of the late 1800s. Some of them live in scattered settlements, far from urban centers, and have little contact with the outside world. Most caiçaras who have traditional lifestyles live along the southeast Atlantic coast. Their primary crop is manioc, which they process into flour.

Some caboclos also have traditional lifestyles. They might do small-scale farming in the Amazon forest, where they raise manioc, corn, rice, beans, and watermelon. Some collect fruits from papaya and other trees and fish in the rivers and streams. Others are *seringueiros*, or rubber tappers. Still others rely on collecting Brazil nuts. To protect their activities, caboclos have formed workers' associations and also take part in local environmental politics. They work on government-approved reserves, which they agree to manage in an environmentally sustainable way.

Rubber tappers carefully cut into rubber trees so the latex drains out. The latex is used to make rubber.

Indigenous Lifestyles

The traditional lifeways among the Indians of the Amazon vary from group to group. Nevertheless, many aspects of daily life are similar for them all. Indians build homes of wood with layers of palm leaves for the roof. One house may be home to several extended families. These homes are often temporary shelters, as families move to different hunting locations during the year. Homes near the rivers are built high on stilts. This keeps the residents safe from floods during the rainy season.

Men go out hunting in groups. They bring their sons, training them to hunt forest animals with bows and arrows, spears, or blowguns with poison-tipped darts. A peccary or a tapir might feed a family for a day or more. Women teach their daughters to

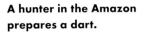

A hunter in the Amazon prepares a dart.

The Xinga people live in houses covered with palm tree leaves.

weave mats or baskets and cook in clay pots over the fire. If the group is cultivating crops, the adults may spend part of the day working in the fields. Survival is serious business, yet the pace of daily life is casual. People rest in the daytime and sleep at night in hammocks strung between two poles.

While this describes a traditional lifestyle, it does not describe the lives of most indigenous Brazilians. The lives of many combine aspects of traditional indigenous ways with typical modern Brazilian life. A 2012 survey of more than 1,200 indigenous people found that 63 percent watch TV, 51 percent own a refrigerator, 37 percent have a DVD player, and 36 percent use cell phones. Some are using modern technology to protect their traditional lands. The organization Amazon Conservation Team is training Indians to use global positioning systems (GPS) and Google Earth to map their territory. So far, they have mapped 70 million acres (28 million hectares) of their rain forest homelands. With these maps, the Indians can identify threats to protected areas.

Eating in Brazil

Brazilians enjoy delicious meals and snacks because they grow so many food crops. Just a few of the locally grown fruits are bananas, papayas, mangoes, guavas, avocados, *pitangas* (large berries), and *amoras* (like blackberries or mulberries). Some local vegetables are *chuchu* (green, fuzzy, and pear-shaped), *jiló* (in the eggplant family), and *maxixe* (in the cucumber family). Cashews and Brazil nuts are local products, too.

Rice, beans, and manioc are staples in the Brazilian diet. Manioc is a root crop that Indians have cultivated for thousands of years. Brazilians typically consume it as *farinha*, or manioc flour, which is sprinkled over rice and beans. Another preparation is *farofa*, made by toasting manioc flour in oil with onions and other ingredients.

Brazil's national dish is a meat and black bean stew called *feijoada* (pronounced fay-ZWAH-dah). It originated among enslaved Africans, who mixed African food traditions with Portuguese foods. Authentic feijoada contains almost any part of a pig—ears, tail, snout, and feet. Over time, changes crept into the recipe. Now feijoada might include smoked sausage, bacon, pork loin, or beef. Typically it is served with farofa.

Many dishes of African origin are popular in the northeast. *Vatapá* is a specialty in Bahia state. It's a shrimp stew with a sauce made of coconut milk, cashews, and red peppers. Vatapá is often stuffed inside a popular street food called *acarajé*. That's black-eyed peas shaped into a ball and deep-fried in palm oil. *Churrasco* is a favorite in southern Brazil. It consists of meat arranged on skewers and barbecued on a grill. Again,

Let's Make Feijoada!

Feijoada, Brazil's national dish, is a pork stew with black beans. This is an easy version of the recipe. Be sure to have an adult help you.

Ingredients

4 cloves garlic	14 oz. pork sausages
1 large onion	24 oz. pork tenderloin
¼ cup green onion	56 oz. canned black beans (can sizes may vary)
¼ cup cilantro	Water
1 large tomato	6 bay leaves
3 tablespoons olive oil	Salt
16 oz. thick bacon	Pepper

Directions

Chop the garlic, onion, green onion, cilantro, and tomato. Put 2 tablespoons oil in a cooking pot, add the chopped ingredients, and cook for about 15 minutes. Chop the bacon, slice the sausage, and cube the pork tenderloin. One at a time, brown the meats in a frying pan with 1 tablespoon of oil. Add the browned meat to the cooking pot and cook for 10 minutes. Mix in the beans. Add enough water to cover the beans. Bring to a boil on high heat and then lower the heat to medium. Add the bay leaves and the amount of salt and pepper you prefer. Cook until most of the water is boiled away, stirring frequently so the beans don't burn. Serves 8.

farofa is the usual side dish. It's common for people to invite friends over for churrasco on a Sunday afternoon.

In the cities, people shop at farmers' markets called *feiras*. There they can get fresh fruits and vegetables, meat and fish, cheese, deep-fried meat pastries, coconut water, and sugarcane juice. For breakfast, Brazilians typically eat bread and butter washed down by coffee mixed with hot milk. Some people also eat fruit, such as papaya, and cold meats. The traditional time for the midday meal is around 1:00 p.m. It is the main meal of the day, with pasta or feijoada, dessert or fruit, and *cafezinho*, which is strong Brazilian coffee. However, working people without much time to spare are more likely to grab a

Brazilians drink more coffee per person than people in almost every other country in the world.

quick lunch at a food stall or fast-food restaurant. Dinner is served around 8:00 p.m., and is usually a simple meal. It might consist of leftovers, or soup, bread, or cold cuts.

In Brazil, the average elementary school class has twenty-five students.

Going to School

The school year in Brazil lasts from February through December, with the month of July off. Children in Brazil are required to go to school from ages six through fourteen. Still, many children from poor families attend only four years of school or even less. They need to work to help support their families.

Playing Queimada

Queimada, meaning "burned," is a favorite children's game in Brazil. It's played on a court, a field, or some other rectangular area. Players are divided into two teams, each grouped on one half of the court. Each end of the court is marked off as the "cemetery." One player from each team stands in the cemetery on the other team's side.

To begin, the cemetery player tosses a ball to his or her team on the opposite side of the court. Whoever catches the ball throws it across at the opposing team, trying to hit a player. If the ball touches someone, that player "dies" and must go to the cemetery on the other team's side. When everyone on one team has gone to the cemetery, that team loses and the game is over.

Each city arranges its own daily school schedule, so there is a lot of variation in school hours. In rural farming areas, school is organized around sowing and harvest times. Generally, the school day lasts only about four hours, with a short break for lunch. Some students might attend morning sessions, from around 7:00 a.m. until 12:00 p.m. Others may attend school in the afternoon, beginning at noon or 2:30 p.m. Some schools even have an evening session. This schedule allows flexibility for students who work.

Primary school lasts nine years, split into two sections—grades 1 through 5 and grades 6 through 9. The core subjects are Portuguese language, history, geography, science, math,

The law school at the University of São Paulo is the oldest law school in Brazil. It was established in 1827.

and physical education. In the upper grades, students study a foreign language such as English or Spanish. Students may go on to a three-year secondary school, which covers ages fifteen to seventeen. They can take courses that lead either to college or to a profession. Brazil has dozens of colleges and universities. The largest is the University of São Paulo. Free public schools are available, but students whose parents can afford the tuition attend private schools.

After school, kids might take part in school-sponsored sports, music, or dance programs. They might go to the beach, fly kites, see a movie, or play computer games. Playtime activities may differ among children from wealthy, middle-class, or poor families. But one pastime seems to cut across all levels of society—soccer! Whether players take to a regulation soccer court or a patch of dirt, the joy of the game is the same. Go Brazil!—*Vai Brasil!*

Timeline

Indigenous people live in Brazil. **9000** BCE

ca. 2500 BCE   The Egyptians build the pyramids and the Sphinx in Giza.

ca. 563 BCE   The Buddha is born in India.

313 CE   The Roman emperor Constantine legalizes Christianity.

610   The Prophet Muhammad begins preaching a new religion called Islam.

1054   The Eastern (Orthodox) and Western (Roman Catholic) Churches break apart.

1095   The Crusades begin.

1215   King John seals the Magna Carta.

1300s   The Renaissance begins in Italy.

1347   The plague sweeps through Europe.

1453   Ottoman Turks capture Constantinople, conquering the Byzantine Empire.

1492   Columbus arrives in North America.

Portuguese explorer Pedro Álvares Cabral reaches Brazil and claims it for Portugal. **1500** CE

1500s   Reformers break away from the Catholic Church, and Protestantism is born.

Portuguese colonists establish their first settlement, São Vicente. **1532**

Missionaries establish São Paulo. **1554**

Portuguese settlers found Rio de Janeiro. **1565**

Miners discover gold in Minas Gerais. **ca. 1695**

Almost one million enslaved Africans live in Brazil. **1700**

Diamonds are found in Minas Gerais. **1729**

BRAZILIAN HISTORY

WORLD HISTORY

1776	The U.S. Declaration of Independence is signed.
1789	The French Revolution begins.

Brazil gains independence from Portugal. **1822**

1865	The American Civil War ends.

Brazil outlaws slavery. **1888**

1879	The first practical lightbulb is invented.

Emperor Pedro II is deposed; **1889**
Brazil becomes a republic.

1914	World War I begins.
1917	The Bolshevik Revolution brings communism to Russia.
1929	A worldwide economic depression begins.

A revolt puts Getúlio Vargas in power. **1930**

1939	World War II begins.
1945	World War II ends.

The capital of Brazil moves from **1960**
Rio de Janeiro to Brasília.

Xingu National Park is established as **1961**
Brazil's first indigenous reserve.

Military dictatorship begins. **1964**

1969	Humans land on the Moon.

Civilian rule returns. **1985**

1975	The Vietnam War ends.
1989	The Berlin Wall is torn down as communism crumbles in Eastern Europe.
1991	The Soviet Union breaks into separate states.
2001	Terrorists attack the World Trade Center in New York City and the Pentagon near Washington, D.C.

Luiz Inácio Lula da Silva of Brazil's **2003**
Workers' Party becomes president.

2004	A tsunami in the Indian Ocean destroys coastlines in Africa, India, and Southeast Asia.

Dilma Rousseff is elected Brazil's **2010**
first female president.

2008	The United States elects its first African American president.

Brazil to host soccer's World Cup. **2014**

Fast Facts

Official name: Federative Republic of Brazil

Capital: Brasília

Official language: Portuguese

São Paulo

Brazilian flag

Official religion:	None
National anthem:	"Hino Nacional Brasileiro" ("Brazilian National Anthem")
Type of government:	Federal republic
Head of state:	President
Head of government:	President
Area:	3,287,612 square miles (8,514,876 sq km)
Latitude and longitude of geographic center:	10°S, 55°W
Bordering countries:	Venezuela, Guyana, Suriname, and French Guiana to the north; Colombia to the northwest; Peru and Bolivia to the west; Paraguay and Argentina to the southwest; and Uruguay to the south
Highest elevation:	Neblina Peak, 9,888 feet (3,014 m) above sea level
Lowest elevation:	Sea level along the coast
Average high temperature:	In Rio de Janeiro, 85°F (29°C) in January; 78°F (25°C) in July
Average low temperature:	In Rio de Janeiro, 74°F (23°C) in January; 65°F (18°C) in July
Average annual rainfall:	46 inches (117 cm) in Rio de Janeiro; more than 160 inches (400 cm) in the western Amazon

Fernando de Noronha island

Rio de Janeiro

Currency

National population (2012 est.): 193,946,886

Population of major cities (2012 est.):

São Paulo	11,376,685
Rio de Janeiro	6,390,290
Salvador	2,710,965
Brasília	2,645,532
Fortaleza	2,500,194

Landmarks:
- ▶ *Christ the Redeemer statue*, Corcovado Mountain, Rio de Janeiro
- ▶ *Iguaçu Falls*, Paraná border with Argentina
- ▶ *Sanctuary of Bom Jesus do Congonhas*, south of Belo Horizonte
- ▶ *Sugar Loaf Mountain*, Rio de Janeiro
- ▶ *Teatro Amazonas*, Manaus

Economy: Coffee is Brazil's major crop and most valuable agricultural export. Soybeans, wheat, sugarcane, and rice are also important crops. Leading factory goods include textiles, shoes, chemicals, cement, cars and car parts, aircraft, and other transportation equipment. Brazil also has valuable natural resources such as iron ore, bauxite, gold, petroleum, lumber, and water for hydroelectric power.

Currency: The real. In 2013, US$1 equaled R$1.97, and R$1 equaled US$0.51.

System of weights and measures: Metric system

Literacy rate (2011): 90%

Schoolchildren

Jorge Amado

Common Portuguese words and phrases:

Oi.	Hello.
Muito obrigado.	Thank you very much.
De nada.	You're welcome.
Não entendi.	I don't understand.
Bom dia.	Good morning.
Boa tarde.	Good afternoon/evening.
Boa noite.	Good night.
Tchau.	Good-bye.

Prominent Brazilians:

Jorge Amado (1912–2001)
Novelist and political activist

João Gilberto (1931–)
Musician

Joaquim Maria Machado de Assis (1839–1908)
Poet and novelist

Oscar Niemeyer (1907–2012)
Architect

Pedro II (1825–1891)
Emperor

Pelé (Edson Arantes do Nascimento) (1940–)
Soccer player

Cândido Portinari (1903–1962)
Artist

Dilma Rousseff (1947–)
President

Heitor Villa-Lobos (1887–1959)
Music composer and conductor

To Find Out More

Books

▶ Barber, Nicola. *Brazil*. New York: Franklin Watts, 2010.

▶ Buckley, James. *Pelé*. New York: DK Publishing, 2007.

▶ Deckker, Zilah. *Brazil*. Washington, DC: National Geographic Children's Books, 2008.

DVDs

▶ *Discovery Atlas: Brazil Revealed.* Discovery Channel, 2007.

▶ *Families of the World: Families of Brazil.* Master Communications, 2010.

▶ *Into the Wild—Jungle Journey: Living with an Isolated Amazon Tribe*. ABC News, 2010.

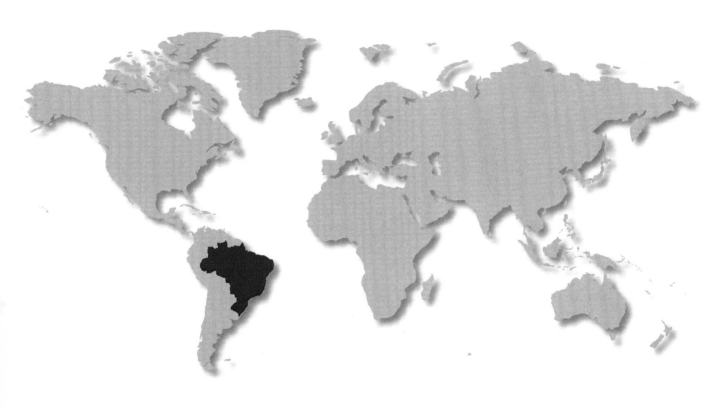

▶ Visit this Scholastic Web site for more information on Brazil:
www.factsfornow.scholastic.com
Enter the keyword Brazil

Index

Page numbers in *italics* indicate illustrations.

Meet the Author

Ann Heinrichs begins to get itchy if she hasn't been out of the country for a while. She has traveled through much of Europe, as well as the Middle East, East Asia, and Africa. Writing about other countries and cultures keeps her in touch with places she's visited and those she hopes to visit someday.

Heinrichs grew up roaming the woods of Arkansas. Now she lives in Chicago, Illinois. She has written more than two hundred books for children and young adults on American, European, Asian, and African history and culture. Some of her other titles in the Enchantment of the World series are *Greece*, *Japan*, *Egypt*, *Niger*, *Nigeria*, *Ethiopia*, and *Wales*. Several of her books have won state and national awards.

"When I'm starting a country book," says Heinrichs, "I head for the library's reference department. Some of my must-see resources are *Europa World Year Book* and the periodicals databases. For this book, I also read online issues of the *Rio Times* and other newspapers to get a feel for Brazilians' current interests and viewpoints. The Brazilian government's statistics Web site was very helpful, and so were United Nations sites such as UNESCO, UNICEF, and the Human Development Reports."

Heinrichs would rather write nonfiction than fiction. "I guess I'm a frustrated journalist," she says. "I'm driven to track down facts and present them in an engaging way. For me, facts are more exciting than fiction, and I want my readers to experience a subject as passionately as I do. Also, I feel it's vital for American kids to understand unfamiliar cultures, so I like to report on what kids in another country are doing—to tell about their interests, values, and daily lives, as well as their economic role in the family."

Photo Credits